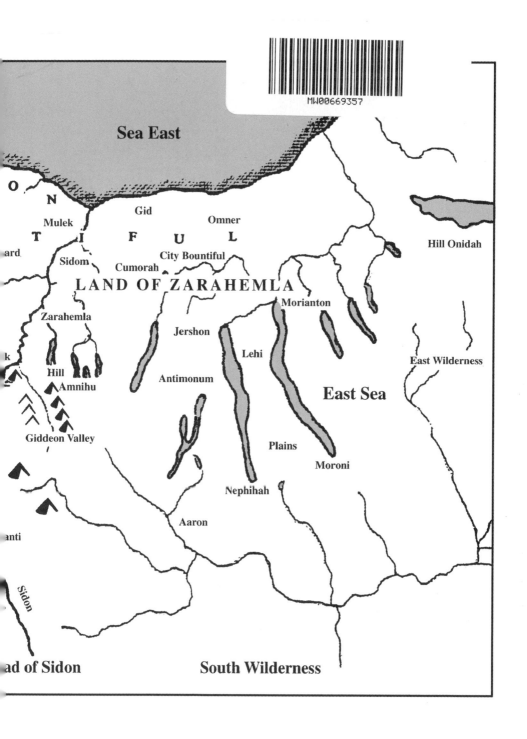

Proposed Geographical Setting for The Book of Mormon

Return to CUMORAH

Library of Congress Catalog Card Number 96-86571
ISBN 0-9655167-0-9

Second printing, May 2003

Return to CUMORAH

DUANE R. ASTON, PH.D.

American River Publications
Sacramento, California

Acknowledgments

The first draft manuscript for this book was produced in 1991. Dr. T. Eugene Shoemaker, Professor of Government at my university and a devout Latter-day Saint friend, became excited over my ideas on a New York geographic setting for the Book of Mormon. Later he wrote the Foreword to this book and passed away before it could be published. His sustained love and support will never be forgotten.

The following manuscript readers made helpful suggestions on the structure, organization and contents in the development of this book. They are: Robin White, Dawn Jones Brown, Sandra Lundquist, John Clark, Dean Thompson, Chris Mackay, Paul Steed, Steven Seither, Perrianne and Paul Allen, Elaine Schlegel, Lynn Jones, Shirley Webb, Bonnie Mitchell, and Kim McCall. Many thanks goes to Jack Lyon for his editorial suggestions in earlier manuscript versions.

Other who assisted in matters related to the production of this book were Jared White, Ana Mae DeWalt, Berenice Young, Joan Criddle, and Elaine Hinds.

Special thanks are expressed to Jennifer Utley for her commitment and for managing the final production of this book.

I am most grateful to my wife Connie for her continued editorial reviews over the years, for her love, support, and inspiration, and to all the members of my family who have sustained excitement about this writing project. Special recognition goes to my parents Ralph and Til for their undying encouragement.

Contents

Chapters

Foreword

THE MAJOR THESIS OF THIS WORK IS THAT BOOK OF Mormon geographers by and large have looked for the wrong things in the wrong places. The author invites all to consider his research and his findings with the possibility that a Book of Mormon geography can be more accurately and faithfully determined.

His years of studying and analyzing the evidence as it has emerged has produced the volume which you hold in your hands. In some ways it is monumental, a treasure of research findings. One's mental impressions will be forever changed as familiar passages are reread in new and plausible geographic settings.

The reader will be powerfully moved by a more faithful reading of Book of Mormon text that speaks of the travels, wars, fortifications, and the beautiful verdant setting in which these people lived and worshiped God.

Most exciting to this reader is the careful research and the faithful use of the text for more accurate and plausible locations of landmarks as guide to the placement of cities and other artifacts spoken of in the Book of Mormon.

T. Eugene Shoemaker, Ph.D.

List of Maps

List of Pictures and Illustrations

Chapter 1

Those Intriguing Ruins

ARTFUL SKETCHES CAPTURED THE SPLENDOR OF A LOST civilization found in Central America when published by Stephens and Catherwood in 1841.[1] Pictured were crumbling stone temples with rubble lying buried in an entanglement of vines and dense jungle undergrowth. Who were the people of this mysterious civilization, and what had happened to them?

These sketches reached Latter-day Saints in Nauvoo in late 1841. It was soon inferred that the lost civilization must have been left there by people of the Book of Mormon. Thus began a Latter-day Saint involvement with Central America that has persisted to this day.

In the era of the 1950s and 1960s, it would probably be safe to say that nothing had captured the imagination of the Latter-day Saint mind more than did beautiful colored pictures of ancient ruins and artifacts found in Central and South America.

These pictures appeared in many Church publications, including the *Improvement Era* and the Book of Mormon.[2] Archaeology and the Book of Mormon was a popular topic of discussion and the authenticity of the Book of Mormon was seen to be somehow related to external evidences that included those obtained from archaeology.[3]

Seen in many pictures were beautifully crafted ancient temples, murals painted on temple walls, tablets of stone (stelae), majestic buildings, and exquisite jewelry and plates made of gold. Taken collectively, these things strongly suggested that the ancient peoples of Central and South America were somehow related to those of the Book of Mormon. Consequently, many Latter-day Saints still favor this interpretation, even to this day.

Not any different than most Latter-day Saints, I too was fascinated by all these things and had no difficulty in believing that Book of Mormon events had taken place somewhere in Central America, with its influences reaching elsewhere in the Americas.

As a leader in our Seventies Quorum, along with others I was busy placing thousands of copies of the Book of Mormon in hotels and motels and holding firesides that fostered interest in the Book of Mormon. Colored slides were sometimes shown of the fascinating ancient ruins found in Central America.

One particular stela, discovered in Izapa, Chipas, Mexico, was interpreted as the occasion of Lehi telling of the Tree of Life incident, as recorded in 1 Nephi 8:1–38.[4] This stela became known as the "Lehi Stone" and replicas were made and widely distributed.

It is interesting to observe that today Church publications, for the most part, avoid relating the Book of Mormon to any particular geographic location, although Central American interpretations still persist in some cases.[5]

Startling News

What I read came as a complete shock to me early in 1990. It was then that I learned that a Latter-day Saint author had spent nearly 25 years studying and researching Book of Mormon archaeology related to Central America, but that he had lost his faith in the authenticity of the Book of Mormon. It seems that this man had come to the conclusion that there was nothing to be found in the Central American setting that convinced him that the Book of Mormon belonged there.

Whether this man was a competent archaeologist or not, or whether his conclusions were valid or not, were not the issues for me at the time that I learned of his dilemma. The important thing was that it started me thinking.

Of course one should not expect to find any external evidences, obtained from archaeology, that would "prove" the authenticity of the Book of Mormon, as this man had thought. But my reaction to the whole episode was simply this: assuming this man's findings were valid, what if the Book of Mormon did not belong in Central America? Then if Book of Mormon lands were not located in Central America, then where might they belong?

The only reasonable possible solution that came to my mind was New York. What if the setting for the Book of Mormon was anciently located in the lands that we know as New York? After all, Hill Cumorah is located in western New York, and we know that ancient records were buried there. Might this location serve as a starting point to begin a search for the geography of the Book of Mormon?

The more I studied and researched upon the matter, the more I became convinced that indeed the Book of Mormon itself contained sufficient clues that could resolve the issue of the geography of the Book of Mormon.

At the beginning of my studies, it was recognized that archaeology deals with man-made artifacts, and while they may be an important consideration, first and foremost is the matter of geography.

Features of geography are directly observable and they can be compared with those mentioned in the Book of Mormon.[7] Thus to the degree that correlation exists between features of geography and Book of Mormon accounts, confidence can be established.

Comparisons (typically in the chapter endnotes) will be made between the proposed New York geography outlined in this book and the popularly assumed Mesoamerican setting found in Central America (see Maps of Appendix B). After nearly eight years of research and study, I could see that the puzzle of Book of Mormon geography comes together beautifully through the proposed New York geography. Some of the reasons for this belief will now be presented.

The Importance of Knowing Where

A Gospel Doctrine teacher had been reading accounts found in the Book of Alma, chapter 22, wherein a Lamanite king was describing his lands. The teacher then made the statement: "I don't know why we have so much information concerning Book of Mormon geography that we do not understand. Perhaps someday we will."

This statement reflects that, while many Latter-day Saints have a desire to know where Book of Mormon events took place, they typically believe that the location of Book of Mormon lands cannot be determined with any degree of certainty. Since the early days of the Church it has been speculated that those lands were located somewhere in Central America. Yet Church leaders have traditionally had to discourage interest in Book of Mormon geography because they felt that the matter could not be resolved without leading to confusion.[8]

It is recognized that the Book of Mormon was written to teach important religious truths concerning Jesus Christ and to reveal the principles of his gospel as exemplified historically by the peoples of the Book of Mormon. But this should not be misconstrued to mean that knowing the actual geography of the Book of Mormon is not important.

First of all, why would anyone say that knowing the geographical setting of the Book of Mormon is not important? Consider the same question as it pertains to the Bible. Millions of people have sought to experience the Holy Lands, the Sea of Galilee, the city of Jerusalem, and the Garden of Gethsemane, and other places, as they seek to draw closer to Jesus Christ. It seems that seeing the rivers, lakes, and towns where he walked enhances their sense of the reality of the Savior, thus nurturing a deeper appreciation of his mission, his great sacrifice, his resurrection, and inspiring a deeper love for him.

Why wouldn't it also be similarly desirable to experience the places where Book of Mormon events took place? After all, Latter-day Saints understand that the resurrected Savior visited America in the days of the Nephites. Why would it not also be important to understand just where in America this had occurred? It is the premise of this book that Book of Mormon lands really can be identified, and experienced, if we are but willing to recognize that the Book of Mormon itself contains sufficiently many clues on features of geography that can clear up our understanding.

The trouble is that old attitudes and beliefs may get in the way. For example, many believe that the setting for the Book of Mormon can only be a matter of conjecture. But, while this has been historically the case, must this always be so? Is it possible that the confusion and the speculation historically found can be dispelled by a better understanding of what the Book of Mormon tells us? If so, where do we begin?

We can first recognize that the Hill Cumorah, mentioned in Mormon, Chapter 6, is a point of Book of Mormon geography that should be known with certainty, since the Prophet Joseph Smith and the Saints in the early days of the Church accepted its location as indisputable.[9] Therefore this should be the starting point from which to start to begin building an understanding of Book of Mormon geography.

An attempt will be made in this book to demonstrate that the lands of the Book of Mormon are to be found mainly in the area of western New York, with lands reaching into Canada on the north, and the states of Pennsylvania and Ohio on the south. Needless to say, the Book of Mormon is only an abbreviated account of the Jaredites and the Nephites. Just how far beyond these proposed lands peoples of the Book of Mormon spread out is left for readers to contemplate.

Christ's Church Restored

In support of a New York geography for the Book of Mormon, is it not fitting that the restoration of Christ's church occurred within those same Nephite lands wherein dwelt a remnant of the seed of Lehi? Recall that the disciples of Christ formed a church of Christ among the Nephites in all the lands, shortly after the visit of the Savior (4 Nephi 1:1). It seems appropriate that when Christ's church was restored in 1830, this restoration had occurred within those same Nephite lands, wherein was to be found Lamanite descendants.

A few months later in 1830, the first mission of the Church began "into the wilderness among the Lamanites" with Indians then living in western New York (D&C 32:2). Thus the Lord's promise to the seed of Jacob was fulfilled, that he would establish his church among them, to whom he had given "this land for their inheritance" (3 Nephi 21:22, 23).

A Land of Promise and Liberty

The Lord showed Nephi that "many multitudes of Gentiles" would come "upon the land of promise." These Gentiles would "prosper and obtain the land for their inheritance." These Gentiles would be "fair and beautiful." They had "gone forth out of captivity," having the power of the Lord with them (1 Nephi 13:14–16). What other people could this refer to, other than those Gentiles, pilgrims, who had come to occupy eastern United States and Canada in colonial times?

The Lord promised Lehi that this land of promise, "a land choice above all other lands," was to be not only for Lehi and his seed, but also for "all those who should be led out of other countries by the hand of the Lord." This land was to be "a land of liberty" (2 Nephi 1:5, 7).

Found in New York Harbor is a great statue standing 305 feet tall, The Statue of Liberty, signaling to all the peoples of the world since 1884, including those coming from Central and South America, that the United States is indeed a land of liberty. The inscription at its base beckons to all by its inscription, "Give me your tired, your poor, your huddled masses yearning to breathe free . . . " ("The New Colossus" by Emma Lazarus, 1883).

Nowhere else is there a nation in the Americas that Gentiles have flowed unto, a nation that has historically stood for liberty, more than is the case for the United States. Some historians believe that the form of government of the Five Nations of the Iroquois (possibly the seed of Lehi) of western New York likely served as a model of democracy to the designers of the U.S. Constitution.[10] If Book of Mormon lands are indeed to be found as proposed in this book, then these ideas take on special significance as they pertain to the nation of the United States.

It will be the objective of this book to demonstrate that these lands found in eastern United States and Canada were those lands wherein Book of Mormon events took place.

Endnotes
(see Bibliography for references)

1. Stephens (1969).
2. The Book of Mormon (Salt Lake City: Deseret Book Co., 1950). This edition of the Book of Mormon contained full colored photographs of temples, an astronomical observatory, pyramids, palaces, and carved stelae. Also included were artful textiles, murals on temple walls showing light and dark skinned people, gold objects, and jewelry.
3. Talmage (1952), 273–274. In this reference, it is stated that "the authenticity of the Book of Mormon constitutes our most important consideration of the work...not only does the Book of Mormon merit such consideration, it claims, even demands the same." In addition to evident truth contained therein, "to these may be added certain external, or extra-scriptural evidences, amongst which are; corroborative testimony furnished by archaeology and ethnology."
4. The Book of Mormon (Salt Lake City: Deseret Book Co., 1950), 344. The Book of Mormon interpretation of this stela offered by Wells Jakeman is certainly interesting. However, considering that people of Mediterranean origins quite likely came to the Central Americas in prehistoric times offers other considerations. The tree of life episode, given in the Book of Genesis of the Bible, is seen portrayed not only in Mesopotamia art, but in other art forms found in the Central Americas. It may well be that this stela represents a Garden of Eden tree of life, inasmuch as there are Garden of Eden elements that can be seen in this "Lehi" stela. For example, in the Garden of Eden there was a tree, fruit, a serpent, a river, Adam and Eve, burnt offerings, and sons Abel (good) and Cain (evil).
5. *The Book of Mormon Student Manual (Religion 121–122)* published by the Church Educational System in 1979 contained 613 pages with many pictures of ruins and artifacts taken from Central and South America, assumed to have a Book of Mormon interpretation. In the 1989 edition of this manual, 184 pages are largely devoid of these kind of pictures, although historical pictures still portray Christ in a tropical, mountainous setting.
6. *Dialogue* (Spring, 1990). Thomas Ferguson published two works: *Ancient America and the Book of Mormon,* and *One Fold and One Shepherd*, in the years 1950 and 1962. In this article it is stated, "believing that he would find the physical proof that would not only justify his faith in the Book of Mormon but that would convince the world as well. This outlook left him vulnerable to disappointment when the evidences and proofs were not to be found where and when he thought they should be." Michael Coe, a noted anthropologist, reported in 1973 that "nothing, absolutely nothing, has ever shown up in any New World excavation which would suggest to a dispassionate observer that the Book of Mormon was a genuine historical document providing information about early peoples of America."
   This article states that "although most competent students of the problem would look to Mesoamerica in general, *the question of the implied geography of the Book of Mormon is far from settled, the diversity of opinions correlating the internal geographical requirements with the external world extends to the present.*"

7. Book of Mormon geographers typically agree that following the great destruction that occurred at the crucifixion of Christ, changes in the land occurred. Yet, Book of Mormon accounts establish that the narrow neck of land was still there, the River Sidon was still there, and the city of Zarahemla, while burned, was still there, etc. It seems that while the "face of the land became deformed," and while cities were sunk in the earth, and "hills and valleys made in the place thereof," the general features of the land remained identifiable (Mormon, Chapters 8 & 9).

8. Reynolds and Sjodahl (1955) states that "attempts that are constantly being made to identify the cities and lands of the Book of Mormon with the old and obscure ruins found in Mexico and points further south, will end in failure." They go on to quote the 1890 views of Elder George Q. Cannon wherein he notes the confusion that has typically occurred in creating maps that show where Book of Mormon events took place. Elder Cannon mentions that for this reason the First Presidency then discouraged pinpointing where Book of Mormon lands were located. He concluded his remarks by noting that, "*at the present time*," such attempts led to confusion and thus were to be discouraged.

9. The Prophet Joseph Smith, in his journal in 1834 described a revelation which was given to him, wherein knowledge was given concerning a certain Lamanite named Zelph (see *History of the Church,* by Joseph Smith, Vol. 2, Deseret Book, p. 79.) The Prophet relates the Zelph account, in terms of an "east sea" (see Map A, on this book cover), a last battle at Hill Cumorah, and a great Prophet "Onondagus" (name of a famous New York Indian tribe). It is particularly important to recognize that this account of the Prophet was given in 1834, years before any notions concerning Central America ever originated. Once ideas on Central America surfaced in matters of Book of Mormon geography, it appears Church historians began to question the Zelph account (see *In Search of Cumorah,* by David Palmer, Horizon Publishers, 74–78). Contrary to what some think, the Zelph account strongly implies that the Prophet Joseph Smith viewed Hill Cumorah in New York as the last battle site of the Nephites.

10. "Some historians claim that the highly democratic political organization of the Iroquois League (the Indians of western New York) may have served as a model for the compilers of the United States Constitution" (Grolier Encyclopedia of Knowledge, 1991, p. 246).

Chapter 2

Hill Cumorah in Central America?

AS THE LIGHTS GO OUT AT THE END OF THE PAGEANT, "America's Witness For Christ," the statue of the Angel Moroni standing high on Hill Cumorah suddenly becomes illuminated by a floodlight at the end of the performance. Viewing this, the audience feels deeply moved by the pageant and senses the importance of this hill as the place where the Prophet Joseph Smith had received ancient records from which the Book of Mormon was translated.

But there is much more to this hill than a pageant, than a place for tourists, than a steep climb up its slope, or even than the inspiring shaft of granite on Cumorah's promontory, upon which the Angel Moroni statue stands. Hill Cumorah bears an important message to give. This book will suggest what that message might be.

After the Church became established in the tops of the Rocky Mountains in Utah, for many decades only a few of the Saints had the opportunity to visit Hill Cumorah. In 1907, Church Historian George

Hill Cumorah as photographed by George E. Anderson.
Copyright the Church of Jesus Christ of Latter-day Saints. Used by permission.

E. Anderson photographed Hill Cumorah. His photograph captured the barren hill, perhaps in much the same way that it might have appeared in the days of the Prophet Joseph Smith.

Site of the Last Battles

The Prophet Mormon hid up in Hill Cumorah all the records in his possession prior to the last battle of the Nephites (Mormon 6:6). The plates used by the Prophet Joseph Smith in the translation of the Book of Mormon are known to have been removed from Hill Cumorah. It is only logical that the Prophet Joseph Smith understood that the Hill Cumorah of New York was that hill mentioned in the Book of Mormon.

Given that the Prophet had this understanding of Hill Cumorah, it would be equally likely that Oliver Cowdery would also have had the same understanding as the Prophet. Oliver played a prominent role in early Church history, being as close to the Prophet as any other man. Oliver's views on Hill Cumorah are presented as follows.

> I think that I am justified in saying that this is the highest hill for
> some distance around, and I am certain that its appearance, as it rises so
> suddenly from a plain on the north, must attract the notice of the travel-
> er as he passes by . . .
>
> At about one mile west rises another ridge of less height, running
> parallel with the former, leaving a beautiful vale between. The soil is of
> the first quality for the country, and under a state of cultivation, which
> gives a prospect at once imposing, when one reflects on the fact, that
> there, between those hills the entire power and national strength of both
> the Jaredites and the Nephites were destroyed.
>
> . . . you will read Mormon's account of the last great struggle of this
> people, as they were encamped round this hill Cumorah. In this valley
> fell the remaining strength and pride of a once powerful people, the
> Nephites . . .
>
> From the top of this hill, Mormon, with a few others, after the battle,
> gazed with horror upon the mangled remains of those who, the day
> before, were filled with anxiety, hope or doubts . . .
>
> This hill, by the Jaredites, was called Ramah: by it, or around it
> pitched the famous army of Coriantumr their tents . . . " "In this same
> spot, in full view from the top of this same hill, one may gaze with aston-
> ishment upon the ground which was twice covered with the dead and
> dying of our fellow men. Here may be seen where once sunk to nought
> the pride and strength of two mighty nations . . . [1]

This account should leave little doubt that the early Saints believed
that the Hill Cumorah was the site of the last battles of both the
Jaredites and Nephites. It appears that most members of the Church
shared this viewpoint for over more than a century following the
death of the Prophet Joseph Smith in 1844.

Speculation Begins

Beginning in about 1841, the Saints in Nauvoo learned that ruins
had been discovered in Yucatan, not far from the Isthmus of Panama,
and it became popular to believe that the Jaredites and the Nephites
had first landed in Central America, and that these peoples had eventually migrated to New York for their last battles at Hill Cumorah.

Nowhere in the Americas had such spectacular ruins been discovered. It was only natural that the early Saints quickly thought the ruins were those of Book of Mormon peoples. However, at that time, the archaeology of Central Americas was only in its infancy.

In the fall of 1842 two editorials appeared in the Church newspaper, the *Times and Seasons*. Inspired by knowledge of these ancient ruins, the author of these editorials strongly supported the idea that the land of Zarahemla must surely have been located in Central America.

Since the Prophet Joseph Smith had editorial responsibility for the *Times and Seasons*, it has since been speculated that either he wrote the articles, or that they had his endorsement.

However, at the time that these editorials were written, the Prophet was in hiding from his enemies, fearful for his life, and his whereabouts was known only to his closest associates. It has never been proven that the Prophet endorsed the idea that the land of Zarahemla was located in Central America. However, in his journal the Prophet did make reference to the ruins as being those of Nephites.[2] But that is a long way from his endorsement that the land of Zarahemla was in Central America.

As it turns out from present-day knowledge in archaeology, the ruins that first excited the Saints were not those of the Nephites.[3] Yet most Book of Mormon scholars today still accept a Mesoamerican setting for the Book of Mormon in Central America, in lands from southern Mexico to Guatamala, mostly excluding the Yucatan Peninsula.

The Sperry Study

It was not until the 1960s that it became clear that the Hill Cumorah of western New York was simply too far from Central America to fit in with the idea that Jaredites and Nephites had landed in Central America and later migrated to New York. In a nutshell, this is what happened.

1. Sidney Sperry made an analysis of the Limhi account wherein an expedition was sent out from the land of Nephi in the south.[4] Their destination was Zarahemla, further to the north. Scholars agree that distance factors would place Zarahemla from one to two hundred miles from the land of Nephi.

2. The expedition over-shot its mark and ended up in a land of many waters where the Jaredites had lived. They found ruins of buildings, hilts of swords, evidences of a terrible destruction, and twenty-four gold plates that were the record of the Jaredites. These artifacts were assumed to have been left by the Jaredites who were destroyed at Hill Cumorah.

3. Thus Sperry's analysis of the Limhi expedition account made it clear that the land of Cumorah must be not all that far from the land of Zarahemla. Since the expedition thought that they had discovered the land of Zarahemla, it can be seen that Cumorah had been rather close to Zarahemla, with the distance measured only in a couple hundreds of miles at most, and not the nearly three thousand miles from Central America to Hill Cumorah in western New York. Other Book of Mormon accounts involving distance factors that Sperry considered are outlined in the chapter endnotes.

The Origin of the Two Cumorah Study

Recognizing the impact of Sperry's findings, Book of Mormon geographers were faced with a dilemma. Either the land of Nephi and Zarahemla were close to Hill Cumorah in New York, or another Hill Cumorah was close to Zarahemla and the land of Nephi in the assumed setting located in Central America.

Instead of accepting that the geography of the Book of Mormon should be associated with the Hill Cumorah of New York, the geographers maintained interest in Central America. Thus it became necessary to theorize that there had to be another Hill Cumorah located somewhere in Central America.[5]

There are probably several reasons why this occurred. First of all, the geographical setting of New York was considered inadequate to support Book of Mormon events. A narrow neck of land near Hill Cumorah was not recognized. Furthermore, it was believed that there were no significant archaeological evidences to be found in western New York.

However, for the purposes of this book, the reasons why geographers have maintained interest in Central America are immaterial. The consequences are inevitable; proposing the existence of another Hill Cumorah somewhere in Central America leads to confusion because most members of the Church know of only one Hill Cumorah.

If there had been another Hill Cumorah, surely the Prophet Joseph Smith would have said so. Why would the hill in New York become known as Hill Cumorah unless the Prophet believed that he had received plates from the Hill Cumorah of the Book of Mormon? The Book of Mormon does not offer even the slightest hint that there could have been another Hill Cumorah, rather it implies that there was only one.

Realizing that the Book of Mormon came forth in 1830 out of western New York at a time when it took no effort to recognize where Hill Cumorah was located, does it not seem perfectly reasonable that this historical landmark was indeed that spoken of in the Book of Mormon, and the place where the Prophet Joseph Smith received ancient plates? Reason dictates that it was.

Placing the lands of the Book of Mormon in Central America creates a need to theorize on the possible existence of a second Hill Cumorah.

The Ancient Records Dilemma

Proposing the existence of a second Hill Cumorah becomes a thorny issue when it comes to dealing with Hill Cumorah as a repository for many ancient records.

When Mormon and his armies marched to the land of Cumorah for their last battles, Mormon "hid up in the hill Cumorah all the records which he had been entrusted," save it were for a few plates that he gave unto his son Moroni (Mormon 6:6).[6]

Proposing a second Hill Cumorah for Central America thus requires one to think that all those records buried there by Mormon are still in Central America. It is theorized that Moroni carried only a small number of records to Hill Cumorah in western New York, those from which the Book of Mormon was obtained.

This is not an acceptable scenario based upon what we know about the Hill Cumorah of western New York for the following reason. Consider an abbreviated account told by President Brigham Young at a conference of the Church in 1877.

When the Prophet Joseph Smith returned plates to Hill Cumorah,

Oliver Cowdery went with the Prophet Joseph when he deposited those plates . . . Oliver says that when Joseph and Oliver went there, the hill opened, and they walked into a cave, in which there was a large and spacious room . . . they laid the plates on a table that stood in the room."

Under this table there was a pile of plates as much as two feet high, and there were altogether in this room more plates than probably more than many wagon loads; and they were piled up in the corners and along the walls.

President Brigham Young further said, "I tell you this as coming not only from Oliver Cowdery, but others who were familiar with it . . . I relate this to you, and I want you to understand it . . . so that they (these things) will not be forgotten and lost."[7]

It would be folly to suggest that, since Brigham Young was an old man when he made these statements, he did not understand nor know what he was talking about.

It seems that Brigham Young's account should be taken in the affirmative that many wagon loads of ancient records lie within the Hill Cumorah of western New York, thus ruling out the possibility of a second Hill Cumorah, as some speculate.

A Matter of Confusion

Speaking on the matter of a possible second Hill Cumorah, Joseph Fielding Smith in 1956 stated that the proposed existence of another Hill Cumorah caused some members of the Church to "become confused and greatly disturbed in their faith in the Book of Mormon."[8]

Apostle Smith then reaffirmed his conviction that Hill Cumorah in New York was the place where the last battles of the Nephites had occurred.

These statements made by Brigham Young and Joseph Fielding Smith have been downplayed by those who persist with ideas on the existence of two Hill Cumorahs.

On the following page is a summary of these idea. Please refer to Illustration 2A (page after) as you read along.

Illustration 2A

The significance of this situation is outlined in Illustration 2A. Please study this illustration in order to obtain the impact of its implication.

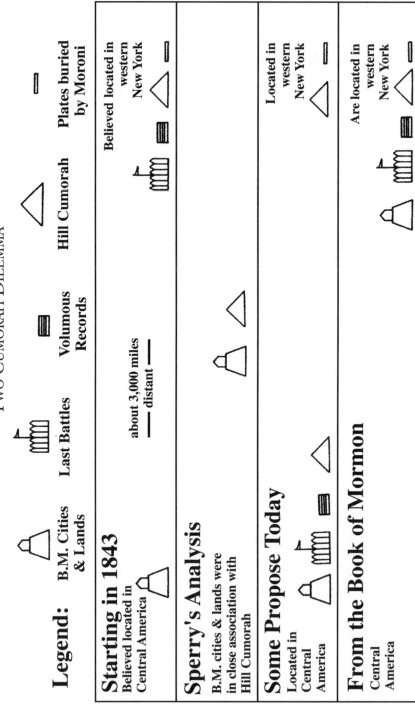

ILLUSTRATION 2A
TWO CUMORAH DILEMMA

16

STARTING IN 1842 it was a popular belief that both Nephites and Jaredites had landed somewhere in Central America, but that these peoples had migrated to Hill Cumorah in western New York. There they fought their last battles, in conformity with Book of Mormon accounts.

SPERRY'S ANALYSIS of the Nephite Limhi expedition made it clear that the distance from the land of Nephi to the land of Zarahemla was probably only a couple hundred miles at most, and that the 3,000 miles to Hill Cumorah in New York was highly improbable. Sperry's study showed that Hill Cumorah was located not far from the land of Zarahemla.

PROPOSED TODAY is the idea that a second Hill Cumorah exists in Central America. There must be volumous ancient records buried there because of great distances involved. Most likely Moroni did not transport many wagon loads of records from Central America to Hill Cumorah in western New York. It has been suggested that Mormon gave only a portion of the plates to his son Moroni so that they could be revealed to the Prophet Joseph Smith and the Book of Mormon translated.

FROM THE BOOK OF MORMON, accounts reveal that the geographic setting for the Book of Mormon is located in the area of western New York. Knowledge of this dispels any need to speculate on the existence of a second Hill Cumorah. The records buried there by Mormon are possibly still contained within this hill, their whereabouts unknown to man until such time as the Lord chooses to reveal them.

When coupled with an understanding that Book of Mormon events did take place in the area of New York, the need for a second Hill Cumorah can be seen to vanish. It remains to be shown, from arguments in geography, that these interpretations are most likely.

Did the Savior visit Central America? What about legends of Quetzacoatl? These and other topics will be discussed later on.

Consequences of One Hill Cumorah

Accepting that Hill Cumorah of western New York is none other than that mentioned in Book of Mormon accounts leads to far-reaching consequences.

This means that Book of Mormon peoples had inhabited the lands associated with this hill, even from the earliest days of both the Jaredites and the Nephites, and that all the Book of Mormon prophets, such as Ether, Lehi, Nephi and others, had lived and moved over these lands.

It also implies that both the Jaredites and the Nephites had sailed from the Old World to somewhere in North America, probably landing on the seashore of what is today the United States or Canada.

This point of view also suggests that the Church of Jesus Christ established by Alma, and the visit of the resurrected Savior to the Nephites had occurred in lands that are today found in the area of western New York.

The destruction that occurred at the time of the crucifixion of Jesus Christ would also be required to have occurred in these lands.

In the chapters that follow, we shall see that the lands described in the Book of Mormon have not been successfully identified in Central America. Evidence appears much more convincing that they are to be found in western New York.

Proposed Book of Mormon Lands

Found on the front inside cover of this book is Map A. Based upon years of thoughtful study, this map is proposed as a plausible interpretation for many interrelated Book of Mormon accounts. All proposed cities and land locations have been analyzed in terms of their compliance with Book of Mormon accounts, correlated with the geographical setting of Map A.

Interested readers may wish to analyze Book of Mormon accounts related to geography (see Appendix B on References in Geography) and to see just how well the cities and lands of this map matches Book of Mormon requirements. In the chapters to follow, some of the reasons for placing cities and land locations on this map will be presented.

Endnotes
(see Bibliography for references)

1. Jessee (1989), 77-79.
2. In the 1842 editorial found in the *Times and Seasons*, it is stated that "the ruins of Zarahemla have been found where the Nephites left them: and that a large stone with engravings upon it, as Mosiah said…we are not going to declare positively that the ruins of Quirigua are those of Zarahemla."

   In his journal (see Joseph Smith, 1978, Vol.5) the Prophet mentions that in consequence of the findings of Stephens and Catherwood, "a large amount of relics of the Nephites, or the ancient inhabitants of America treated in the Book of Mormon, which relics have been landed in New York." It is seen that the Prophet uses the term Nephites in a broad context, as being the ancient inhabitants of America.
3. Allen (1989), 70. "When John Lloyd Stephens reported his archaeological findings in 1841, he emphasized the ruins of Copan, Palenque, and Uxmal. All three are Maya ruins. All three have proven to be post Book of Mormon. This dating does not mean that Classic post Book of Mormon sites were not built upon Preclassic Book of Mormon Time Period sites." From this we can see that today no evidence exists for Nephite occupation on the Yucutan Peninsula.
4. FARMS (SP-WER, 1983). In this publication, Sperry points out that as far back as 1937 it was recognized that the last great battles of the Nephites and Lamanites had taken place near the lands of their early settlements. But the idea was little understood. Following his inquiry, Sperry arrived at the following considerations.

   He points out that Omer (Ether 9:3), early in Jaredite history, passed by hill of Shim, thus establishing that hill Shim could not have been 3,000 miles distant, in New York, from assumed lands in Central America.

   He then recognizes that Coriantumr's last battles occurred near a narrow neck of land (assumed to be in Central America), but that "a few battles later" his armies engaged in their final destruction at Hill Ramah (Cumorah).

   He also recognizes that Coriantumr and his armies were pursuing the armies of Shiz southward, not northward, and if they had been coming up from Central America, this was not possible.

   Then in regards to Limhi's men, he questions if it is reasonable that they would have traveled "three thousand miles (from Central America) to find the site of the last great Jaredite battles" in New York.

   His conclusion was that the "Book of Mormon evidence points inevitably to a Ramah-Cumorah in Middle America."

   Now, if a narrow neck of land had been recognized to exist in western New York, might this have made a difference on Sperry's interpretations? It would seem that not recognizing a narrow neck of land in western New York may have been germane to the origins of the two-Cumorah theory.
5. Palmer (1981, 1992). The dustcover of this book "asserts that the location where the Nephites fought their last battle, the "Hill Cumorah," may actually be el Cerro Vigia, a site located near Mexico's Isthmus of Tehuantepec, just inland from the Gulf of Mexico."

6. FARMS (1992), 17. The plates used in the translation of our Book of Mormon were: the small plates of Nephi, the plates for the words of Mormon, the large plates of Nephi, the plates of Mormon, the plates of Ether, and the plates of Moroni. Some of these plates were abridgements from plates of the record of Lehi, the plates of brass, Benjamin's speech, the record of Zeniff, the records of Alma, the records of the sons of Mosiah, the epistles of Helaman, Pahoran, and Moroni, the records of Nephi, the records of the Jaredites, and the documents from Mormon.

7. Young, *Journal of Discourses*, vol. 19, p. 39.

8. Joseph Fielding Smith (1956) states that "the Prophet Joseph Smith himself is on record, definitely declaring that the present hill called Cumorah to be the exact hill spoken of in the Book of Mormon." He also states that "in light of revelation it is absurd for anyone to maintain that the Nephites and Lamanites did not possess this northern land." These statements of Joseph Fielding Smith are clear that he believed that there cannot be another Hill Cumorah.

Chapter 3

The Narrow Neck

The Neck at Niagara

NIAGARA FALLS ARE WORLD FAMOUS. THESE GREAT WATERS typically capture the minds and hearts of visitors who come from all over the world to witness the spectacle of Niagara's thundering waters. Yet, for most people the meaning of the name "Niagara" is unknown. It sounds Indian, and indeed it is.

But LDS readers will find it quite interesting to learn the meaning of this name. It is derived from the Mohawk tribe of the Iroquois Indians, who occupied nearby lands before the coming of the Europeans.

As it turns out, the narrow neck of land at Niagara has been historically referred to as "the neck" of land, since the days of the early European colonists. Mention of the "neck at Niagara" can be found in pre-Book of Mormon references.[1]

In Appendix B of Schoolcraft's *Notes on the Iroquois* an entry states: "This name is Mohawk. It means, according to Mrs. Kerr, the neck, the term being first applied to the portage, or neck of land, between lakes Erie and Ontario."[2]

The word Niagara probably originated phonetically from two Mohawk words; "ni-waa," meaning small, and the word "on-yara" meaning neck.[3] Thus quite likely the root word "niwaa-onyara" was pronounced Ni-a-gara. The descriptive root "small" has possible added significance.

In the Book of Mormon, Alma 22:32, reference is made to a "*small* neck of land*," while elsewhere reference is made to a "narrow neck" (Alma 63:5), or to "the narrow neck of land" (Ether 10:20).

Significance of the Neck

Regardless of how the small, narrow neck of land at Niagara got its name, there is something quite significant about this neck of land. It makes no difference at all whether the colonists or the Indians referred to this parcel of land as a neck or not. It makes no difference whether the name is Mohawk Indian, or otherwise. The important thing for Latter-day Saints is to recognize that such a narrow neck of land, a small isthmus, exists at Niagara, and that this neck of land has important Book of Mormon consequences.

It is remarkable that a narrow neck of land exists not far from a known point of Book of Mormon geography, the Hill Cumorah. Knowledge of this correlation becomes evidence that the narrow neck of land at Niagara is that neck of land mentioned in the Book of Mormon. So compelling is this knowledge, that it becomes strong evidence that the setting for the Book of Mormon took place in nearby lands. This would seem to go a long way toward dispelling theories that there might exist another Hill Cumorah.[4]

What Is a Neck?

When the colonists came to occupy the coastal lands bordering the Atlantic Ocean, they found small parcels of land that jutted out into the sea and called them a "neck."[5] They were nominally two miles or less across the neck, and extended only a couple of miles or more out into the sea.

The narrow neck at Niagara differs somewhat from these necks. While it is 22 miles across at its narrowest point, the Book of Mormon refers to the narrow neck as being "small" (Alma 22:32). The neck at Niagara is small in the sense that it connects two large land masses, lying between a "land northward" and a land "southward" (see Map A).

Hill Cumorah and the Neck

Accepting that the narrow neck at Niagara and the Hill Cumorah at Palmyra are those mentioned in the Book of Mormon, my attempts at creating a viable map of Book of Mormon geography were hampered by misconceptions that I had picked up from the works of other geographers. I knew that Hill Cumorah of western New York lies below the narrow neck of land at Niagara but was troubled by other geographers who typically place a Hill Cumorah above the narrow neck of land in their maps (see maps of Appendix A).

Prior to their destruction, the Nephites began to "retreat towards the north countries" (Mormon 2:3). Like other geographers, I mistakenly interpreted this to mean lands lying above the narrow neck of land. However, in time I came to realize that there also existed a land lying immediately north of the land of Zarahemla which could be identified as the land Desolation.

The dilemma that I faced was this: if these north countries were above the narrow neck of land as is typically believed, then why do Book of Mormon accounts not give even the slightest hint that Mormon and his armies crossed the narrow neck of land, coming over to the known location of Hill Cumorah for their last battles (see Mormon 6:2)? The record is silent on such a possibility.

This matter disturbed me for years until I was eventually able to shed some new light on the matter. The solution to this puzzle lies in a different understanding of what is meant by use of the term "the land northward."

Simply, it means that almost all significant Book of Mormon events, first involving the Jaredites and then the Nephites, took place in lands located below the narrow neck of land, in lands northward to

Looking northeast from Grimsby Beach near Hamilton,
Toronto lies far to the right on the horizon.
Western Lake Ontario can be considered to be a "sea west."

Looking to northwest from the shore of Lake Erie, a "west sea," below Lake View.
On the horizon, barely visible, is a narrow neck of land.

Zarahemla. The land of Desolation lay on the southern seashores of an ancient lake, present-day Lake Ontario. Evidences for this will be presented in chapters that follow.

In light of the above considerations, and that which will follow, the small neck of land at Niagara and the Hill Cumorah at Palmyra cannot be minimized in importance by students of the Book of Mormon who seek to locate its geographic setting.

Travel across the Neck

Given the above considerations, it stands to reason that both Jaredite and Nephite peoples would have also traveled to lands lying above the narrow neck of land at Niagara, to lands northward from there. They probably crossed the Niagara River using water crafts such as rafts, or small vessels such as the famous light-weight Indian bark canoes. Apparently many Nephites did come to these lands northward, as will be seen.

Crossing the Niagara River by large numbers of native peoples occurred in historic times. It is known that in the 17th century the Huron Indians of Ontario Providence, Canada, crossed the Niagara River by the thousands, and in a series of wars ending in 1654, completely annihilated some 15,000 Eries as a tribe. The Eries had occupied the eastern shores of Lake Erie, spanning from present-day Ohio to the neck at Niagara.

Thus Canadian Indian warriors routinely crossed the Niagara River in their wars. While some portions of the Niagara River cannot be crossed, other portions of the river can be crossed in water crafts.

Thus when the Book of Mormon refers to the land northward, in some cases this reference is relative to lands lying above the narrow neck of land. These interpretations are presented in Map A (see inside front cover of this book).

Lands Northward to the Neck

Following the shoreline of the neck of land at Niagara around and into Canada on the north, the curvature of the lake follows a shoreline border of low-lying lands, that are created by an escarpment ridge. This border consists of lands lying all along the southern shores of Lake Ontario in New York, and stretches northward across the narrow neck of land, into Canada. It seems quite reasonable that both Jaredite and Nephite peoples did make use of these lands located both below and above the narrow neck of land.

Further northward in southern Ontario Providence, exists a land of "large bodies of water and many rivers" (see Helaman 3:4). However, there is another feature of geography associated with these lands northward above the narrow neck that is rather unique.

In this regards, in Helaman 3:8, it is stated that in the land northward the Nephites came to cover the whole earth, "from the sea south to the sea north, from the sea west to the sea east." One might wonder how such a feature of geography could possibly exist, wherein a body of land is completely surrounded by water and not considered an island. So difficult is this specification, that it has been suggested that this description may have been "metaphorical."[6] But is this so?

Please refer to Map 3.1 on the following page, and note that southern Ontario Providence is bordered by four distinctly identifiable bodies of water, or seas. Whether these seas are connected to each other is of no consequence; it is the directional orientation of four bodies of water that best satisfies the description found in Helaman 3:8.

Southern Ontario is bounded by Georgian Bay on the north, by Lake Erie on the south, by Lake Huron on the west, and by Lake Ontario on the east. So distinctive is this feature of geography, that one might wonder where else in the world could such a unique four-sea correspondence be found for a land northward, in close proximity to a narrow neck of land, as mentioned in the Book of Mormon.[7]

While the land northward to the narrow neck at Niagara strongly supports Book of Mormon accounts, there is even more to this neck of land that can be correlated to other Book of Mormon descriptions. Let us now consider what else might be involved with this narrow neck of land.

Where the Sea Divides the Land

The Book of Ether mentions a Hill Ramah, that is identified as the same Hill Cumorah of the Nephites. In the days of Lib, the Jaredites

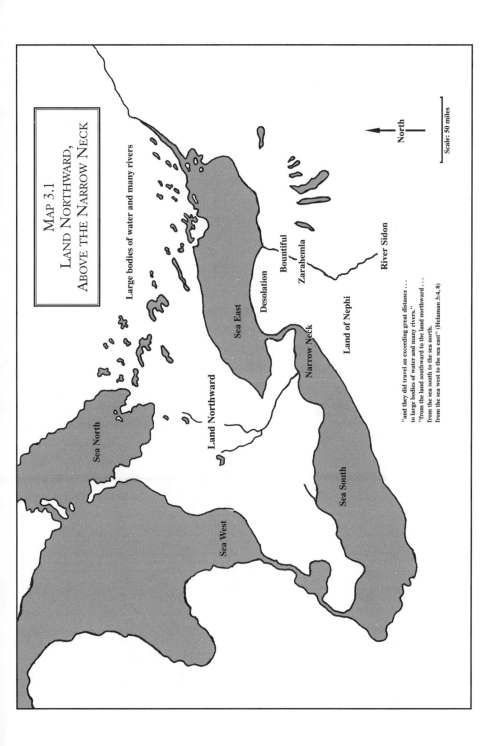

MAP 3.1
LAND NORTHWARD,
ABOVE THE NARROW NECK

Large bodies of water and many rivers

Sea North

Land Northward

Sea East

Sea West

Narrow Neck

Desolation

Bountiful

Zarahemla

Land of Nephi

Sea South

River Sidon

"...and they did travel an exceeding great distance . . .
to large bodies of water and many rivers."

"from the land southward to the land northward . . .
from the sea south to the sea north.
from the sea west to the sea east" (Helaman 3:4, 8)

North

Scale: 50 miles

"built a great city by the narrow neck of land, by the place where the sea divides the land" (Ether 10:20).

The dictionary defines an isthmus as a narrow strip of land having water at each side and connecting two larger bodies of land. At first glance one might think that the narrow neck of land at Niagara qualifies as an isthmus. Yet this strip of land does not connect two larger bodies of land, because it is divided by water!

Looking at a map of the narrow neck at Niagara, one can recognize that the waters of the great Niagara River actually divide the land. How perfect; the narrow neck of land at Niagara also has a "place where the sea divides the land!"

Now, where else in the world is there a more appropriate place, associated with proposed Book of Mormon lands, to find a narrow neck of land where waters from a sea completely divides the land?[8]

Jaredite Waters of Ripliancum

As one contemplates the significance of the narrow neck of land at Niagara, one's mind is drawn to the Niagara River. What a spectacle is seen in its falls that are world famous. Surely somewhere in the Book of Mormon there should be a reference to this great feature of geography because it is so closely associated with the narrow neck of land.

As it turns out, the record of the Jaredites gives us a clue. In the final days of the Jaredites, Coriantumr and his people "came to the waters of Ripliancum, which by interpretation, is large, or to exceed all" (Ether 15:8).

If present Lake Ontario was Ripliancum, then the Niagara River would provide the waters, considered as a fountain, that feeds the large body of water, Ripliancum.

What cinches the matter is the description "large, or to exceed all." True this might be thought to be applicable to just about any other river or source of water, but only when one contemplates the Niagara Falls does it become clear that there is no other river anywhere that can match its majesty.

The Horseshoe Falls is 186 feet high, 2,950 feet across, and carries almost all the waters of the Niagara River. The American Falls is 193 feet high, 1,400 feet across, and carries a smaller portion of the waters of the Niagara River. Combined, these falls pour half a million tons of water per minute into a steep-walled gorge! These falls drain the Great Lakes, the largest body of fresh inland waters found in North America. Millions of visitors have come from the four corners of the world to witness the wonder of the Niagara River. Only when one catches the mist of its falls, feels and hears the deafening roar of its thundering waters, is blown by its strong turbulent winds, then can the Niagara River leave an everlasting impression on the human mind.[10] These waters of Ripliancum are indeed "large…to exceed all."

Hagoth's Ship

In about 53 B.C., Hagoth built a large ship which transported thousands of men, women and children (Alma 63:4–10). The ship was launched into "the west sea, by the narrow neck of land which led into the land northward." This location suggests a western extension of Lake Ontario, a sea on the west by the narrow neck of land, from which they "took their course northward."

This might have involved at least a 30-mile trip across Lake Ontario, which possibly may have landed on shores near the present-day city of Toronto, in Canada.

Ships were possibly used for two purposes. First, to transport wives, and children, those who would find it easier to sail rather than cross the more treacherous river found at the narrow neck (the Niagara River), and take a longer path by land. Second, since the land northward to the narrow neck was "desolate and without timber," the Nephites "did send forth much by the way of shipping" (Helaman 3:10).

Other ships were built and other voyages were made. However, on Hagoth's second voyage, the ship was "never heard of more," and it was supposed that the boat and passengers were "drowned in the depths of the sea."

Thus the Nephites did journey into lands northward above the narrow neck. It included travel by ship, sailing across the "west sea" that borders on the north of the narrow neck.

It is reasonable that the Jaredites also went into lands northward. The desolation of the north lands in Nephite times occurred because of the "many inhabitants who had before inherited the land" (Helaman 3:5). Found in the Book of Ether is mention that Jaredites built a great city, by the narrow neck of land (Ether 10:20.). Suggestions of where this city may have been located will be presented in a later chapter.

Map A suggests that the land northward had two components. First, it existed in lands north of Zarahemla, whereby those Nephites who went to north countries, went directly north until they reached the southern shores of what is today Lake Ontario. Second, these lands bordering the sea extended further north to points into what is today Ontario, Canada.

A Sea on the East and on the West

Accepting that the narrow neck of land was like an isthmus, as such it divides waters on each side of it. The Book of Mormon does not mention the orientation of the seas on either side of the narrow neck. However, one will note that the neck runs west-east, and is surrounded by waters on its north and south. Typically, Book of Mormon geographers envision an isthmus running north-south, with water on the west and east (see Maps Appendix B).

The king of the Lamanites described the lands of his realm in terms of a sea on the east and on the west. Some Book of Mormon geographers have inferred that this was in reference to the narrow neck of land, bounded by a sea on the east and a sea on the west. But is this correct?

Examining what the Lamanite king said, his lands were "in all the regions round about, which (lands) bordered "the sea, on the east and on the west" (east and west extensions of Lake Ontario), which sea "was divided from the land of Zarahemla by a narrow strip of wilderness." More on where this narrow strip of wilderness may have been located will be discussed in another chapter.

But the significant thing here is that there was only one sea involved, and not two as typically inferred. What this account tells us is that there was only one sea (Lake Ontario), but its end portions on the east and west are referred to as the 'sea on the east' and the 'sea on the west.'

Other references are made to a sea, that is quite likely Lake

*Niagara River waters from Lake Erie entering Lake Ontario,
represents "the place where the sea divides the land" (Ether 10:20).
Used with permission of the New York Power Authority*

*A 1776 watercolor sketch of Niagara Falls by Thomas Davies.
Used with permission of the New York Historical Society.*

Ontario. One can see from Map A that "the land of Nephi did run in a straight course, from the east sea (Lake Ontario) to the west" (Alma 50:8). Please notice there is no mention here of a west sea, merely the "west" (Please refer to Map A). However, identifying the land of Nephi involves other considerations that will be presented later on in this book.

In Alma 50:34, mention is made of a "narrow pass which led by the sea, yea, by the sea, on the west and on the east." Again, please note the use of a singular sea. This clearly is another example of a reference to the same sea, with a west and an east extension, likely meaning east and west extensions of Lake Ontario. More on this narrow pass will be presented in a later chapter.

A Land of Many Fountains

As the local merchant handed me my change across the counter of his small store, he responded to my question. Yes, this town of Springwater (near Hemlock Lake) got its name from the springwater that wells up there. Typical homes have water pumps in the basement that can pump out water at the rate of about three to five gallons per minute. However, nobody appreciates this much water. The farmers cannot plow because spring-fed waters soak their fields most of the time.

Water from melting ancient glaciers produced what is seen today as the Finger Lakes of western New York. The longest of these lakes is Cayuga Lake, some forty miles in length. Next in size is Seneca Lake, some thirty-seven miles in length. These lakes are drained by a system of creeks and rivers, that empty into Lake Ontario on the north. Further east, creeks and rivers drain into the Susquehanna and Hudson River systems.

Less than twenty miles north of Canandaigua Lake, third largest of the Finger Lakes, is found the Hill Cumorah at Palmyra. Cumorah is described as a land "of many waters, rivers, and fountains" (Mormon 6:4). Correlation between the lands proposed in Map A and these accounts from the Book of Mormon gives assurance that the Hill Cumorah of western New York matches Book of Mormon accounts.

A view of fertile farm lands typically found in the vicinity of Caledonia, Ontario. It lies in the southwestern end of a narrow neck of land.

The Grand River runs north to south over most of southern Ontario. Here near Caledonia, it lies just west of a narrow neck of land.

*One of three spectacular waterfalls of the Genesee River
found in Letchworth State Park,
about 35 miles south of Rochester, in a land of many waters.*

*A view of north Conesus Lake, near Livonia.
This area, about 25 miles southwest of Palmyra,
was likely part of the land of Zarahemla.*

34

Given the above considerations, one can see that the Hill Cumorah was located to the north, and not far from the land of Zarahemla (see Map A).

In Summary

So striking are the features of geography associated with the Niagara narrow neck of land, in light of what has been presented above, one can only reasonably conclude that this is the narrow neck of land mentioned in the Book of Mormon.

The significance of identifying this important feature of geography has far reaching effects. Importantly, it dispels any notions or ideas that there exists another Hill Cumorah anywhere else except in western New York. It also means that Book of Mormon events occurred in the lands associated with these important features of geography.

As will be shown in the chapters that follow, there are other features of Book of Mormon geography that can now be identified with reasonable assurance.

Readers are invited to explore and contemplate the related matters briefly presented in the Endnotes that follow.

Endnotes
(see Bibliography for references)

1. Wheeler-Voegelin (1974, 15-16); Beauchamp (1968, 288).
2. Schoolcraft (1975, 20).
3. Ibid, Appendix L; vocabularies, taken from letter from Rev. Wm. McMurray, to H.R. Schoolcraft, 1845.
4. Is there a suitable narrow neck of land in Mesoamerica? Most Book of Mormon scholars today consider the Isthmus of Tehauntepec to be the narrow neck of land referred to in the Book of Mormon. However, this isthmus is 125 miles across at its narrowest point. One should have difficulty in seeing this neck as being "small," as specified in Alma 22:32.

    Proposed Nephite lands typically do not involve the Yucatan Peninsula in any significant way. Thus one might wonder in what sense the Isthmus of

Tehauntepec would appear "narrow" for a proposed Nephite geography that is as wide as the neck of land itself (see Maps Appendix B).

5. In New York there is Great Neck, Thong's Neck, Eaton's Neck, and Crane Neck. In Connecticut there is Giant's Neck and in Massachusetts there is Little Neck and Castle Neck. Typically these necks are two miles or less across the neck.

6. F.A.R.M.S. (1989, 65).

7. Most Book of Mormon geographers accept the Isthmus of Tehauntepec as the narrow neck of land. However, this neck of land is bounded by two bodies of water; the Gulf of Mexico northward, and the Pacific Ocean southward. It obviously has no identifiable sea on either the east or the west (see Maps Appendix B).

These two bodies of water cannot satisfactorily satisfy the Four Sea specifications mentioned in Helaman 3:8 regarding a land northward to the neck.

Another consideration is that the land northward to the neck of land had "many large bodies of water and many rivers" (Helaman 3:4). The land northward to the Isthmus of Tehauntepec has a few rivers, but it lacks large bodies of water.

8. The Isthmus of Tehauntepec, if considered as a narrow neck of land, has no feature of geography wherein one could find a place where the sea divides the land.

9. Following their wandering in the wilderness, Lehi and his family came to the shores of a sea that they called "Irreantum," which is interpreted as "many waters" (1 Nephi 17:5). Thus a sea may be referred to as "waters," and if the sea is large like an ocean, it would be "many waters." When the Jaredites came to the "waters of Ripliancum," this most likely referred to a sea named Ripliancum. Recall that the "waters of Mormon" were a "fountain of pure water" (Mosiah 18:8). Thus the "waters of Ripliancum" most likely refer to waters that acted like a fountain, or source of water for Ripliancum. In this sense, one can see that the "waters of Ripliancum" were quite possibly the waters of the Niagara River, acting as a fountain or source for the sea Ripliancum. If this is so, there is not a better candidate for these waters that could be considered to be "large, or to exceed all," as a fountain or source.

10. Some Book of Mormon geographers identify a great swamp and lagoon system of waters of Central Veracruz as a possible "waters of Ripliancum." If these were the waters of Ripliancum, then why can one find other similar waters a couple hundred miles or so to the east that are greater in magnitude? Thus the proposed waters of Ripliancum are in violation of the requirement that they be considered large enough to "exceed all."

Chapter 4

The River Sidon

A T THE AIRPORT, ONE OF MY TWO SUITCASES CONTAINED a small two-man tent. Plans called for me to camp out in the backwoods, rural areas found in New York, Pennsylvania, Ohio, and Canada. My itinerary called for me to travel far and wide in exploring features of geography and the lay of the land which I believed might be related to accounts found in the Book of Mormon.

The purpose of the tent was for convenience in late evening lodging in mostly farming areas where hotel or motel accommodations would be hard to find. I was amused and actually delighted at the idea of pitching my tent, as was the practice of the peoples of the Book of Mormon. My years of camping experience as a scout leader came in handy.

The jumbo jet broke through the clouds and banked as I got a first aerial view of the historic water falls at Rochester. My immediate reaction was that the Hill Cumorah near Palmyra was indeed located in a land of "many waters, rivers, and fountains," as mentioned in the Book of Mormon (Mormon 6:4).

This trip was a follow-up to studies I had made that convinced me that the lands of the Book of Mormon are to be found in the vicinity of western New York and Canada. How far they may have extended into neighboring states, and into Canada, remained to be determined.

As far as landscape goes, a hill is just a hill. However, I recognized that no armchair understanding of any proposed geography would do. Even topographical maps found in libraries had their limitations. I had to see for myself points of geographical interest.

Although I had visited the western New York area at various times in the past, there were many aspects of its geography of which I had little knowledge. Through the explorations of this field trip and one other that occurred two years later, I eventually came to a better understanding of the topography of the area.

For the following discussion, please refer to Maps A and B found on the inside front and back covers of this book.

The River Sidon

A study of maps of western New York had convinced me that the Genesee River was most likely the River Sidon of the Book of Mormon. By heading southward from the city of Rochester, following the concourse of this river, it was easy to understand why this might be so.

The northern reaches of the Genesee River are probably among the most agriculturally fertile areas found in western New York. Seen from 435 miles into space, a modern full-color satellite map reveals areas of agricultural development which clearly illustrates this.[1] Here the river valley is very broad in places. Such fertile lands bordering this river could have easily provided abundant crops of corn, wheat and barley grown by the Nephites (Mosiah 9:9).

Toward the south, the river valleys become very narrow and steep hills dominate the landscape. Further south, across the Pennsylvania border, the Genesee River has a head that lies just north of a dense national forest. This strongly hilly area is not prone to agriculture, and thus the wilderness area found at the head of the Genesee River has been preserved.

The Genesee River is the longest river in western New York, with its head waters located about 110 miles (as the crow flies) in southern highlands, near Gold, Pennsylvania. From there it flows northward, emptying into Lake Ontario, which can be considered as a sea on the north. River Sidon is generally believed to have terminated in a sea on the north (see maps of Appendix A).

From an analysis of Book of Mormon accounts, geographers seem to generally agree that the River Sidon flowed from southern highlands, to the north, or from "up" to "down." This is also the case for the Genesee River. Both rivers empty into a sea on the north, and both rivers possess a rather distinct wilderness area associated with their headwaters.

The Land of Zarahemla

The village of Geneseo lies about 30 miles south of the city of Rochester, and west of the northern reaches of the first of the Finger Lakes, namely Conesus Lake, Hemlock Lake, Canadice Lake, and Honeoye Lake. Spanning east and west above these lakes is today a region of extensive agricultural activity.

Book of Mormon accounts mention that the "borders of Zarahemla" were lands which were "by the waters of Sidon," in a "land southward which had become covered with buildings, and the people were as numerous almost as it were the sands of the sea" (Mormon 1:6–10). As illustrated in Map A, please notice that the proposed land of Zarahemla lies southward from lands bordering along a southern seashore, which is identified as a "land northward" relative to Zarahemla.

The area around these lakes is known to have once had a heavy concentration of Indian villages, many of them fortified, suggesting the high desirability of this area for human habitation, possibly reaching far back into Nephite times.

It is possible that the city of Zarahemla had once existed somewhere on the Genesee River in about this vicinity.

The Land of Zarahemla became the hub of Nephite activity, dating from the days when King Mosiah left the land of Nephi and discovered the people of Zarahemla who had first come to these lands where Mosiah discovered them (Omni 1:12–16). While actual distances are not specified in locating the land of Zarahemla on the River

*The Genesee River is an excellent candidate for the River Sidon,
seen here from the campus of the University of Rochester.*

*Looking northeast from near the village of Naples,
this is a view into lands which may have been part of the land of Zarahemla.*

Sidon, agricultural considerations seem to suggest its proposed location on Map A.

Proximity of the Genesee River to the known Hill Cumorah in the north would seem to suggest that this river was indeed the River Sidon of the Book of Mormon. If so, then the Hill Cumorah was near events associated with the land of Zarahemla. Again, in Alma 2:15 it is noted that the River Sidon ran by the land of Zarahemla.

Referring to the internal maps of Appendix A, please notice that other geographers typically place Hill Cumorah outside of the core of Book of Mormon events, in a land that seems too far northward, too far from the core of Book of Mormon events which occurred at Zarahemla.

It would seem that only the proposed New York geography can make it clear that Hill Cumorah was indeed located not far from the heart of Book of Mormon events. Perhaps for this reason Hill Cumorah was chosen as the site for the last battles of both the Jaredites and the Nephites.

Gideon Valley / Hill Amnihu

Just south of the village of Geneseo a broad valley forks off from the Genesee River toward the southeast, running for about 15 miles, to the present village of Danville. This valley, about two miles in width, is an excellent candidate for Gideon Valley (Alma 2:20).

Seen bounding this valley on the east of the Genesee River, is a high hill. This hill is broad on top, spanning the length of the entire valley, and is a good candidate for the Hill Amnihu (Alma 2:15).

The Book of Mormon mentions that to the east of the River Sidon was a Hill Amnihu. This hill was the location where 6,562 Nephites and 12,532 Amlicites were slain in fierce battles that lasted all day (Alma 2:15–19). The hill bordering the east of the valley at Danville rises steeply, and is long and broad enough on its upper reaches where thousands of Nephites and Amlicites could have battled.

Alma gave up pursuit of the Amlicites and his people then pitched their tents in the valley of Gideon (Alma 2:20), suggesting that the valley of Gideon must have been nearby Hill Amnihu.

After the Nephites "departed out of the valley of Gideon toward their city, which was the city of Zarahemla," while crossing the River

Sidon they were attacked and tens of thousands of Lamanites and Amilcites were slain. The people of Nephi pursued them "west and north" toward the wilderness called the Hermounts (Alma 2:26–37).

Later Alma departed from the city of Zarahemla, and "went over upon the east of the River Sidon, into the valley of Gideon" (Alma 6:7–8). In the city of Gideon Alma declared the word of God to the church there.

A Valley Path to the South

In Alma 16:6–7 it is found that Zoram and his sons "marched away beyond the borders of Manti into the south wilderness, which was on the east side of the River Sidon." Most Book of Mormon geographers recognize that the land of Manti lay on the southern reaches of the River Sidon (see Maps, Appendix A).

Please refer to Map A and note that both the proposed Gideon Valley and the River Sidon lead southward to the land of Manti. Because of the rugged terrain afforded by the deep canyons of the proposed River Sidon in this vicinity, it is possible that Nephite journeys southward were routed through Gideon Valley, rather than following the rugged and difficult course of the River Sidon.

Consider Alma 17:1, wherein it is recorded that "Alma was journeying from the land of Gideon southward, away to the land of Manti." Thus it is possible that Alma, like other travelers, chose to journey through Gideon Valley to reach points southward from Zarahemla.

Thus the valley at Danville seems to match Book of Mormon accounts quite well. The proposed site for this valley is located in close proximity to the site proposed where the city of Zarahemla may have been located.

The Hermounts

In the vicinity of the village of Geneseo, on the west are a series of ranges of high hills, running north-south, which might be identified as the Hermounts mentioned in the Book of Mormon. According to Book of Mormon accounts, the Hermounts lay north and west of the

River Sidon, in relation to the valley of Gideon (Alma 2:37).

The Hermounts was a "wilderness which was infested by wild and ravenous beasts" (Alma 2:37). The Seneca Indian Museum at Salamanca, contains life-like stuffed animals that include ferocious bears, wolves, and wildcats that once inhabited the forests of western New York. One would have no difficulty in identifying these animals as the ravenous beasts.

The Book of Mormon relates that the Hermounts were west and north of the heart of the land of Zarahemla. On this most scholars seem to agree (see maps of Appendix A).

The relationship between the valley at Danville, containing a broad hilltop of sufficient size and length, located east of the Genesee River just south of Geneseo, and a high mountainous region to the north and the west of Geneseo, seem to correspond very well with Book of Mormon requirements for Gideon Valley, Hill Amnihu, and the Hermounts.

The Banks of Sidon

Just south of Geneseo, the Genesee River enters a very deep chasm consisting of steep cliffs. This area is designated today as Letchworth State Park. It represents some 14,300 acres of wilderness area. Its natural beauty includes three beautiful waterfalls and a forested area containing nearly vertical cliffs, reaching heights of 600 feet.

The breathtaking steepness of these cliffs might remind one of the banks associated with River Sidon in Book of Mormon accounts. The Nephites fought with and slew Lamanites and Amlicites upon the west bank of River Sidon (Alma 2:34; 3:3). Please note that this occurred as the Lamanites were fleeing into the wilderness of the Hermounts.

Thus according to Map A, the Lamanites who were slain upon the bank of Sidon may have been caught there because of the steepness of the banks in this vicinity of the river (43: 40, 51). It is interesting to contemplate why Lamanites would be slain upon the banks of any river unless the banks were so steep that they presented a barrier, or if the river was too deep and swift to cross for easy passage.

Other Nephite accounts refer to Lamanites crossing River Sidon, gathering in the valley, upon the bank of Sidon (see Alma 43:40–42, 51). Thus in other locations the river may have been bordered by the flat lands of a valley. This is true of the Genesee River valleys further south from the Letchworth State Park area.

Today a road sign just outside of Letchworth State Park carries the name, "Highbanks."

The Head of Sidon

Traveling southward from Geneseo, following the course of the Genesee River, one eventually reaches the village of Gold, Pennsylvania, where the head of the Genesee River is located. Here the highlands reach their apex, dropping to lower elevations on all sides of the divide upon which the head of Sidon is located.

In Alma 22:29 it is stated that the Lamanites occupied the wilderness area just south of the head of Sidon. Thus the head of Sidon lay on a line of demarkation, perhaps the natural divide of the land, between the Lamanites and the Nephites.

In Alma 56:25 mention is made that the Lamanites used the head of Sidon in their west to east movements of their armies. This was likely because the Lamanites stayed within the wilderness areas south of the head of Sidon to avoid detection by the Nephites.

Thus the head of the River Sidon, because of its location, may have been a key point for the Nephites to monitor movements of the Lamanites.

The South Wilderness

Continuing further south beyond the head of the Genesee River, in Pennsylvania, one enters a region of steep canyons and rugged forest lands. Today these are lands designated as state forests. These lands are known to have once been dense hardwood forests. Near the New York border, within Tioga State Forest, is found the famous "Grand Canyon of Pennsylvania," about twenty-five miles southeast of the head of the Genesee River. Steep tree covered cliffs drop off dramatically into Pine Creek that snakes its way along, far below.

Originating near the head of the Genesee River is the Cowanesque

*The valley of Danville, east of the Genesee River, may have been Gideon Valley;
a candidate for Hill Amnihu is seen.*

*West of the village of Geneseo is a high range of hills running north to south,
a good candidate for the Hermounts.*

River, which flows eastward. Also originating near the head is the Oswayo River, which flows westward. In Nephite times, Nephite populations likely existed along these water ways "from the east to the west" (Alma 22:29), thus creating a line of occupation which separated the Nephites on the north from the Lamanites in the south wilderness areas.

The existence of heavily forested areas today in national forests just south of the head of the Genesee River, make it easy to imagine just what kind of a wilderness may have existed below the head of the River Sidon in Nephite times. In traveling through these forested areas today, one can better appreciate the wilderness areas mentioned in the Book of Mormon.

A Parting View

These are only a few points of geography that I first observed in my journey through what I believed to be Book of Mormon lands. After nearly 3,000 miles of travel through these lands, camping along the way, my plane headed for home. As it climbed into the clouds, seen on the hazy southern horizon, lay a land beyond that I believed was the ancient land of Nephi.

My hope was that someday I might share with others some the experiences that I obtained there. Later on I again returned to these special lands for further explorations.

In Summary

The Genesee River is indeed a good candidate for the River Sidon. Its proximity to the Hill Cumorah, and its correspondences with Book of Mormon accounts, is reassuring. While it is true that there are other rivers in the general area that could be considered, including the Niagara River, none of these other potential candidate rivers can match Book of Mormon specifications as well as does the Genesee River.

The highbanks of the Genesee River in Letchworth State Park may have been part of the wilderness which divided the land of Nephi from Zarahemla.

Found today is the densely wooded area near the head of the Genesee River, likely the south wilderness below the head of River Sidon.

Endnote
(see Bibliography for references)

1. Advanced Satellite Productions Inc., Richmond, BC, Canada, May 28, 1989. Distributed by Bookmarks, Corning, N.Y.

Chapter 5

The Mysterious Line

JUST HOW FAR MIGHT ONE SUPPOSE THAT A NEPHITE would travel in a day and a half's journey? Under normal circumstances he would most likely walk, and not run. While there is no definite answer to this question, finding a reasonable answer is of importance because such a distance is specified for the length of a "line," a feature of geography mentioned in Book of Mormon accounts.

In about B.C. 80, it was stated that; "And now, it was only the distance of a day and a half's journey for a Nephite, on the line Bountiful and Desolation, from the east to the west sea" (Alma 22:32).

Whatever the "line" was, it must have been important because it apparently formed some kind of a boundary between the lands of Desolation and Bountiful.

As it turns out, this reference in geography proved to be one of the most interesting and puzzling pieces related to the geography of the Book of Mormon. Its mystery was finally solved for reasons which will be explained as follows.

The Dilemma of Desolation

The root of the matter lies in understanding the correct location for the lands of Desolation and Bountiful mentioned in the Book of Mormon. Surprisingly the dilemma occurred because historically Book of Mormon geographers have made some incorrect assumptions regarding where the lands of Desolation and Bountiful were located.

The land of Desolation got its name because it had once been occupied by numerous Jaredites, whose wars and destruction had left the land desolate (Alma 22:30). Jaredite accounts mention the narrow neck of land and a land northward (Ether 10:20–21). Thus the assumption was made that the land Desolation lay north of the narrow neck of land, with Bountiful to the south (see Maps of Appendix A).

Some geographers propose that the line, a "day and a half's journey for a Nephite," represented the distance across the narrow neck of land, from one sea to the other, dividing Desolation on the north from Bountiful on the south.[1] However, the line had nothing to do with the width of the narrow neck of land, as will be shown.

Consider now two other important references to the "line."

In the 57th year (B.C. 38), the Nephites were defending their lands against the Lamanites. It is stated that they "did fortify against the Lamanites, from the west sea, even unto the east; it being a day's journey for a Nephite, on the line which they had stationed their armies to defend their north countries" (Helaman 4:7).

In the year A.D.17, Nephites were again defending their lands. They had "gathered themselves together, to defend themselves against their enemies. And the land which was appointed was the land of Zarahemla and the land Bountiful, yea, to the line which was between the land Bountiful and the land Desolation" (3 Nephi 3:22–23).

A Feature of Geography

Since the line was a place where Nephites "stationed their armies," it must have been rather well defined because it formed a line between the land of Bountiful and the land Desolation. Even if the line consisted of a line of fortifications, perhaps earthen enclosures with timbers, this line of defense could have been constructed on a natural boundary between Bountiful and Desolation.[2]

Another consideration is the nearly 100 years spanned by the dates given in the aforementioned accounts. Whatever fortifications may have been involved, the line was recognized as a boundary between Desolation and Bountiful for nearly a century. Perhaps fortifications were constructed on this line, but it seems that mention of the line over a period of a century would strongly imply that the line was a feature of geography. Since the line retained its usefulness in defense over a long period of time, this implies there was something about the nature of the line that gave natural advantage over enemies.

The Quest for Desolation

Given that the Hill Cumorah of western New York played an important role in Jaredite accounts, and assuming that the Jaredites had occupied lands northward above the narrow neck of land at Niagara, they would be required to eventually travel to Hill Cumorah for their destruction. Then why does the Book of Ether not indicate that Jaredites had ever crossed the narrow neck of land in their final wars?

This disparity suggested to me that the land of Desolation lay below the narrow neck of land, and not above as many believe. But at that point in time, I had no idea of just what the line might have been.

My quest began by a careful reading of the Book of Ether, and a study of features of geography to be found in western New York, looking for a feature of geography that I felt might be a clue for what the "line" was.

It seemed that by placing the lands of Desolation and Bountiful due north from Zarahemla, the dilemma might be resolved. As "north countries," Jaredite lands would be more in keeping with directions mentioned in Helaman 4:7.

The "line" was eventually identified as the Niagara Escarpment, a ridge that traverses across western New York, from the east to a west sea. While this Escarpment also extended northward above the narrow neck at Niagara, into what is today Ontario, Canada, the Book of Mormon seemed to indicate that Jaredite events mainly took place below the narrow neck of land.

While it appeared that the Niagara Escarpment may well have

been the "line," the possibility remained for further investigation. The next task was to see if the escarpment ridge, as a "line," could meet the distance requirement.

Line Distance Estimated

The idea of measuring distances by how far a person could walk has probably been around for ages. Who knows just how far back into time such a practice may have existed?

As the practice pertains to the "line" mentioned in Alma 22, one might begin by trying to find how far Indians typically traveled in one day, in hope that it might give some idea as to how far a Nephite might have traveled in a day.

In colonial times, the early settlers bargained with the Indians for their lands in terms of the distance that a person could travel within a day's journey. Boundaries typically involved rivers, sometimes also referred to as a "line."[3]

William Penn's "Walking Purchase" of 1686 involved Indian lands lying west of the Delaware River, to the Lehigh River. This distance was nominally 40 miles at it's widest points. In this purchase, "the Indians relinquished all the land between the Delaware and Lehigh rivers, that could be traversed in a white man's leisurely day and a half's stroll."[4]

However, after 1737 the colonist's "fleetest runner" expanded the lands of the treaty by running 60 miles in the day and a half. Given this, it would not be unreasonable to say that a Nephite just might travel about 50 miles in a day and a half's journey.

The account in Helaman 4:7 states that the Nephites fortified a portion of the line, a "day's journey for a Nephite." Thus while the line's length was a day and a half's journey for a Nephite, the fortified portion was a day's journey for a Nephite.

Thus two thirds of the line was fortified. Perhaps the western portion of the Escarpment, near the narrow neck of land, was where that fortification had occurred. The proximity of this portion of the "line" would give easy access to the west sea, where the Niagara River empties into Lake Ontario.

It is proposed that the Nephites built cities in the land of

The Escarpment ridge is cut by the Niagara River
forming a deep gorge (at the tower on the left).
East of here, it was a line of fortifications in pre-historic times.

The Escarpment ridge, near the village of Ridgeway on Route 104,
is barely visible at this point, the southern border of the land of Desolation.

Desolation, north of the Niagara Escarpment, in lands bordering the narrow neck. Where those cities might have been located will be considered in more detail in the next chapter.

How might the "day and a half" distance apply to the "line" between the land Bountiful and the land Desolation?

Can the length of the Niagara Escarpment match this distance requirement?

Application to Escarpment

The Niagara Escarpment of western New York apparently created a southern "line" for the land of Desolation because it formed a natural boundary, one which afforded a natural line of demarkation for fortifications against enemies.

The Niagara River, emerging from its gorge, becomes very wide and flows seven miles north to the sea. Here at the gorge, the Escarpment on the New York side has its starting point for the line. From Lake Ontario to the Escarpment, the wide Niagara River can be considered as an inlet to the sea, thus qualifying it as the "west sea," where the line began.

Running eastward from the Niagara River, the Escarpment is a natural ridge that divides the land. The ridge at the Niagara gorge is nearly 200 feet high. Northward from the Escarpment, lands gently slope seven miles down to the seashore of Lake Ontario.

From the Niagara River to points eastward, the ridge gradually diminishes in height to where it becomes barely visible. In that sense, the line basically disappears. Present-day Route 104 passes along this ancient ridge, and villages on this route bear names such as Ridgewood and Ridgeway (see Map B).

The readily observable length of this ridge is about 45–50 miles, thus qualifying it for a "day and a half's journey for a Nephite" along this line, as specified in Alma 22:32.

With this new understanding of the line, came a new meaning for the land northward, and a location for the land of Desolation.

Thus the land of Desolation was an approximately eight to ten mile wide strip of borderlands lying on the southern shore of a sea on the north (Lake Ontario), bounded on the south by a ridge. It was into this long and rather narrow, fertile, seashore borderland that the Jaredites built their cities, and where Nephites also came to live.

In Nephite times, Lamanite armies eventually drove the Nephites into this area, prior to their destruction. From this area both the Jaredites and the Nephites fought their way eastward to hill Ramah/Cumorah, where both peoples were destroyed, at two different time periods.

Why Hill Ramah/Cumorah as the last battle site? A reasonable explanation will be presented later on in this book.

A Highly Visible Line

Please refer to Map 5.1 presented on the next page. This is a construct of a shaded relief map for western New York, taken from a portion of a map by the U.S. Geological Survey.[5] The Canadian portion has been added to outline the neck at Niagara. This escarpment ridge, extending from New York northward into Canada, has been known as the Niagara Escarpment since colonial times. This ridge served not only the Indians, but the colonists as well for a route of travel.[6]

Given that the meaning of the "line" has been found, then an important feature of Book of Mormon geography has been identified, which is peculiar to the proposed New York geography. However, there are other important consequences to be considered, in relation to this proposed "line."

Mulekites Inherited Jaredite Lands

If the Jaredites did inhabit lands bordering along the southern shores of what is today Lake Ontario, this brings their civilization closer to the land of Zarahemla in that their lands were located below the narrow neck of land. There is another important consequence that follows if Jaredite lands were in closer proximity to Zarahemla.

There was a relationship between the lands of the Mulekites and the Jaredites that seems little understood. The prophet Ether prophesied that unless Coriantumr and his household repented, "another people" [the Mulekites] would receive Coriantumr's land "for their inheritance," and that "Coriantumr should receive a burial by them

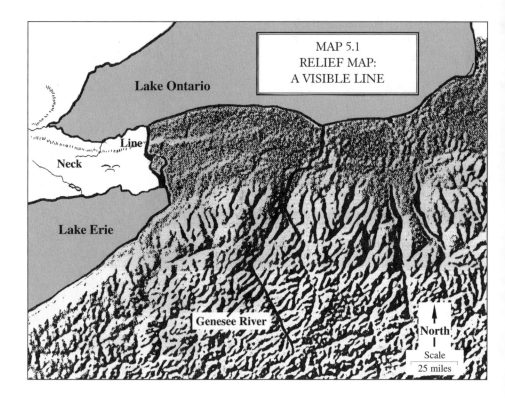

[the Mulekites]; and every soul should be destroyed save it were Coriantumr" (Ether 13:21). Since Coriantumr was discovered by the people of Zarahemla (Omni 21), he was most likely buried by them. This means that it is likely that the Mulekites came to possess the lands of the Jaredites, probably lands lying northward from Zarahemla.

Now, this is something to consider. Since the Lord brought the Mulekites "into the land where Mosiah discovered them" (in Zarahemla) and "they had dwelt there from that time forth" (Omni 1:16, 17), it is clear that the Mulekites always occupied Jaredite lands.

From these considerations, it seems that realizing the geography of the Book of Mormon was centered in western New York has led to some surprisingly different interpretations of Book of Mormon accounts.

Iroquois National Wildlife Preserve, near Batavia.
Wild animals, fish and fowl of very kind, occupy this Bountiful wilderness today.

Indian Falls, located on the Tonawanda Indian reservation.
These lands may have been part of the western portions of the land Bountiful.

Last Battles of the Jaredites

Please refer to Map 5.2. This map was devised from a careful analysis of the battles of Coriantumr and Shiz in the last days of the Jaredites, correlated with the Book of Ether, chapters 13–15. Wilderness areas, mountainous regions, rivers, and the plains were all considerations in geography.

Readers are urged to refer to this map as accounts in the Book of Ether are read and contemplated. This map demonstrates that it is certainly possible that the Jaredites did occupy lands northward from Zarahemla, below the narrow neck of land, south of the shores of an ancient sea, Ripliancum.

A series of final battles involving Coriantumr, Shared, Lib and Shiz occurred. But it was after Shiz "pursued Coriantumr eastward, even to the borders of the seashore," that the tide of the battle changed, and Coriantumr's direction was reversed, causing him to pursue Shiz westward, until they eventually reached the "waters of Ripliancum."

From there, Shiz fled southward to Ogath, while Coriantumr's army pitched their tents northward from there, "by the Hill Ramah (Cumorah)." It was there, at Hill Ramah, that the last battles of the Jaredites were fought.

The destruction was so complete and final, that all had fallen by the sword. After Coriantumr had smote off the head of Shiz, he was the sole survivor of the battles (Ether 15:29), and Ether lived to record what had happened. Ether hid the records such that the people of Limhi could find them (Ether 15:33).

Were all the Jaredites destroyed at Hill Ramah/Cumorah? In Ether 15:12 it is stated that the Jaredites did "gather together all people upon all the face of the land, who had not been slain, save it was Ether." "Wives and their children—both men, women and children being armed with weapons of war...did march forth one against another to battle" (Ether 15:15). Ether had warned that "every soul should be destroyed save it were Coriantumr" (Ether 13:21).[7]

The destruction of the Jaredites at Hill Ramah was complete, and final. Coriantumr was discovered by the people of Zarahemla [Mulekites] and lived with them for a period of "nine moons" (Omni 21).

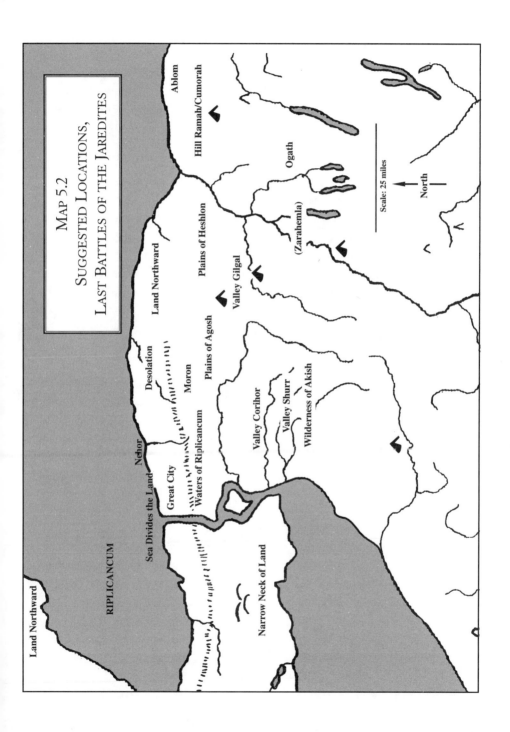

MAP 5.2
SUGGESTED LOCATIONS,
LAST BATTLES OF THE JAREDITES

Ablom

Hill Ramah/Cumorah

Ogath

Plains of Heshlon

(Zarahemla)

Valley Gilgal

Land Northward

Plains of Agosh

Desolation

Moron

Nehor

Great City

Valley Corihor

Waters of Riplicancum

Valley Shurr

Wilderness of Akish

Sea Divides the Land

RIPLICANCUM

Land Northward

Narrow Neck of Land

Scale: 25 miles

North

Archaeological Evidences?

It appears that the Niagara escarpment ridge of western New York makes an excellent candidate for the "line" mentioned in Alma 22. Yet, the question remains: is there any kind of evidence that might demonstrate that an ancient people, had once inhabited the southern shores of what is today Lake Ontario?

Establishing that the "line" is located in western New York has far reaching consequences. Referring to Map A, not only does the identification of the "line" suggest where the lands of Desolation and Bountiful were located, but its singular nature and its precise correspondence with Book of Mormon accounts leaves little room for doubt that the "line" is indeed the one spoken of in the Book of Mormon.

In the next chapter the matter of the "line" will be further explored to see if the archaeological record supports this line, indicating that it had once been an ancient line of fortifications.

Endnote
(see Bibliography for references)

1. F.A.R.M.S. (1992, 187). See Chapter 53, "A Day and a Half's Journey for a Nephite." In this reference, it is assumed that the day and a half's journey for a Nephite had occurred across the Isthmus at Tehauntepec. It is explained how this 120 mile wide neck of land might match Alma 22:32.

2. One geographer (Hauck, 1988, 35-40) points out that "scholars have been so tied to an isthmus explanation that they have not grasped the book's more specific geography." Hauck proposes a narrow neck of land in Mesoamerica that is not an isthmus, but is a narrow coastal section of land instead.

   Pointing out that no east sea is mentioned in Alma 22:32, Hauck proposes a coastal path along an escarpment range of mountains for the "line Bountiful." However, for the scenario proposed, the land Desolation does not lie "northward" of the land Bountiful, and the land Bountiful is hardly "southward" at all, being more like 300 miles to the east. The "line" Bountiful/Desolation is proposed as a distance of fortification, and not as the actual length of the line itself as specified in Alma 22:32.

3. Schoolcraft, vol.1 (1885, 85). In this reference, it is mentioned that the Indians defined "a day's march" as the distance between two rivers, the St. Croix and the Rum Rivers, both found in Minnesota. Also, this account uses the term "line" in referring to St. Peter's River, now called the Minnesota River.

4. Schoolcraft (1885, 85).

   How did the name for the Lehigh River come about? In *Pennsylvania Place Names*, by A. Howry Espenshade (Baltimore: Genealogical Publishing Company, 1970), p. 122, it is mentioned that the Delaware Indians called the Lehigh river the Le-chau-we-kink, "where there are forks." Thus the name may not have been of Indian origin.

5. Thelin & Pike, U. S. Geological Survey, 1991, Map I-2206.

6. Thompson (1966).

7. Proponents of Mesoamerican geography for the Book of Mormon believe that the ancient Olmec civilization of Vera Cruz in southern Mexico were the Jaredites. However, there is a serious problem with this in that while the Book of Mormon relates that the Jaredites were killed off, the Olmec culture is known to have continued on beyond any time period suitable for the Jaredites. Thus it becomes necessary for these geographers to postulate the existence of "Jaredite survivors" (Sorenson, 1985, 119); (Palmer, 1981, 141).

Chapter 6

The Fortified Narrow Pass

IN THE LAST CHAPTER AN EXCELLENT CANDIDATE FOR the "line" mentioned in Alma 22:32 was established. The Niagara Escarpment Ridge spans from the broad Niagara River, seen as a west sea, eastward for approximately fifty miles. This ridge represents a distance that a Nephite could reasonably travel in a day and a half along the "line."

Not only was this natural ridge used for fortification, but it was also used as a corridor for travel. It is referred to as a "narrow pass" in several Book of Mormon accounts.

Thus the Niagara Escarpment ridge was a natural highway, not only used by Book of Mormon peoples, and by later generations of Indians, but it was also used by the colonists in the settlement of western New York, from Rochester to Buffalo. Archaeologists today refer to this escarpment ridge as the "Strand Line."

A modern road map shows that Route 104 threads its way along this escarpment ridge, providing modern travelers a country-side view of the fertile lands lying northward to the shores of Lake Ontario (see Map B).

The Narrow Pass

That the "line" of fortifications was also a "narrow pass" can be seen from the following considerations.

This narrow pass "led by the sea, yea, by the sea on the west and on the east" (Alma 50:34), just as does the escarpment ridge. Please notice that this account refers to a single sea. However, considering that the sea is in reference to Lake Ontario of today, one can note that this account is referring to the east and west extensions of this sea.

The Nephites did "fortify the land Bountiful and secure the narrow pass which led into the land northward...lest the Lamanites should obtain that point and should have power to harass them on every side" (Alma 52:9). This is consistent with "the land northward" lying north above the Escarpment ridge, bordering the southern shore of Lake Ontario.

The Nephites had "lands of our inheritance divided. And the Lamanites did give unto us the land northward, yea, even to the narrow passage which led into the land southward. And we did give unto the Lamanites all the land southward" (Mormon 2:29).

Now if this narrow passage lay along the escarpment ridge, along the "line," it would be a natural line of demarkation, and its fortifications would act as a buffer to keep the Lamanites in the land southward. Thus Nephite lands lying northward to the sea would be protected.

The Nephites "...did gather themselves...at the land Desolation to a city which was in the borders, by the narrow pass which led into land southward" (Mormon 3:5). The borders referred to were most likely those lands lying between the Escarpment ridge, and the seashore of southern Lake Ontario, a sea on the north of Desolation (see Map A).

Since the Escarpment ridge extends from western New York up into Canada, Map A suggests that the land Desolation may have also extended to lands lying above the narrow neck of land, where both Jaredites and Nephites had come to live.

Evidence for Desolation

One consequence of understanding the meaning of the "line" in the New York geography is that it proposes a new understanding for the relationship between the lands of Desolation and Bountiful, and their relationship to the narrow neck of land and the land of Zarahemla. However, is there any evidence that ancient peoples had ever occupied the southern shores of Lake Ontario?

As it turns out, evidence can be found that implies that this lakeshore border was once populated by pre-historic peoples, who had lived there and left behind a great number of former occupation sites. Consulting the 1930 work of H. C. Shetrone on the Moundbuilders, one can find a map of sites that indicates a former heavy inhabitation of the southern shores of Lake Ontario.[1]

Please refer to Map 6.1, found on the following page.

The Ancient "Ridge"

McGavin and Bean, in their 1949 *Geography of the Book of Mormon*,[2] cite the opinions of O. Turner regarding ancient fortification sites that had once existed in western New York:

"On the south side of the *ridge* [Escarpment] nearest the lake…and on the hills in the vicinity, are to be found remains of *fortifications*, yet north of the *ridge* and beyond to the lake-shore, not a single fort is to be found, thus indicating that the *fortified ridge* marked the ancient shore of Lake Ontario, where perhaps 2,000 years ago, a great battle was fought."[3]

They also refer to John McIntosh on the subject:

"The *border* of the lake is the very place that would be selected for habitation and consequently for works of defense…on account of the facilities it would afford for sustenance.'"[4]

Thus the ridge itself was a line of fortifications, while the eight-mile wide strip of fertile lands, extending some 50 miles west to east, provided sustenance for inhabitation. Today, these proposed lands lying north of the escarpment ridge are covered with extensive farming. Much fruit is grown in this region as well.

McGavin and Bean drew their own conclusions regarding the escarpment ridge, found south of the shores of Lake Ontario:

"Many historians have called attention to the high *ridge* that once formed the southern boundary of the ancient lake, which was lined with ruins of ancient *fortifications*. These authorities agree that while

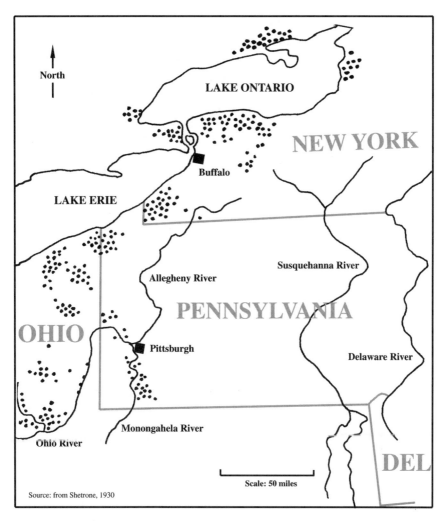

MAP 6.1
ANCIENT OCCUPATION SITES,
INCLUDING DESOLATION

this lake had reached its extreme dimensions, its shores bathing the land far beyond its present limits, an ancient people engaged in a bitter and destructive warfare. At that time *Ripliancum* would certainly describe the huge body of water which served as the northern defense which would protect their rear as they prepared to defend themselves against a powerful enemy."[5]

These accounts make it clear that the early colonists first found numerous ancient fortifications existing along the old ridge "narrow pass," the Niagara Escarpment. This fortified ridge fits the description of the "line" mentioned in the Book of Mormon. McGavin and Bean are fully aware of the fortifications found on this ridge, suggesting that they believed these fortifications were built by the Nephites.

According to the Book of Mormon interpretations presented thus far, the Jaredites occupied the land of Desolation above the "line," separating it from the land of Bountiful just southward. Their destruction may have occurred just prior to the arrival of the Nephites.

However, all accounts that refer to a "line" of fortification were those of the Nephites, who defended their land northward above this "line." Thus while the Jaredites had occupied the land of Desolation first, they were followed by the Nephites who later occupied this land northward, above the "line," and built fortifications to defend it from the Lamanites who came from the south, from the land of Zarahemla.

A Recognized Line

It is remarkable indeed that today archaeologists of western New York refer to the Niagara Escarpment as being the "Strand Line."

Archaeologists today recognize several things about this proposed "fortified ridge," the "line" that is interpreted here as separating Bountiful and Desolation. The following points give some idea of what is believed.[6]

First of all, almost all of the sites illustrated on Map 6.1 have been destroyed in colonial times. Today only a very few sites remain, and they are badly damaged. Most of the ridge lands were put into farm lands and houses built over the original archaeological sites.[7]

A few fortification sites studied by archaeologists have been radio-carbon dated to only 1,000 years ago, and are thought to be the works of the Iroquois Indians, noted for their works of defense.

A few other sites have been dated to times more in keeping with the time period of the Jaredites.

Much could be speculated on concerning the sites illustrated in Map 6.1. It is certainly possible that many of the original sites may

*The escarpment ends abruptly at the Niagara River with 200 foot cliffs.
Here the river is narrow and could be crossed in simple water crafts.*

*After emerging from the gorge, here the Niagara River quickly broadens out,
and in the next seven miles it is like a narrow bay of a west sea.*

have been the work of both Jaredites and Nephites. Perhaps these Book of Mormon peoples left their earthworks standing there, and they were taken over by later generations of warring Lamanites, who installed new wooden fortifications upon the same old earthen sites.

Ancient Sites of Fortification

Historian John McIntosh describes what the ancient and numerous fortifications were like.

> These forts were, generally speaking, erected on the most commanding ground. The walls and breastworks were earthen. The ditches were on the exterior of the works. On some of the parapets, oak trees were to be seen, which, from the number of concentric circles, must have been standing one hundred and fifty, two hundred and sixty, and three hundred years; and there were evident indications, not only that they had sprung up since the erection of those works, but that they were at least a second growth.
>
> The trenches were in some cases deep and wide, and in others shallow and narrow; and the breastworks varied in altitude from three to eight feet. They sometimes had one and sometimes two entrances, as was to be inferred from no ditch at those places. When the works were protected by a deep ravine, or a stream of water, no ditch was to be seen. The area of these forts varied from two to six acres; and the form was generally an irregular ellipsis; and in some of them fragments of earthware and pulverized substances, supposed to have been originally human bones were to be found.
>
> These fortifications, thus diffused over the interior of our country, have been generally considered as surpassing the skill, patience and industry of the Indian race; and various hypothesis have been advanced to prove them of European origin...
>
> It is generally clear that they are not the work of the Indians. Until the Senecas, who are renowned for their national vanity, had seen the attention of the Americans attracted to these erections and invented the fabulous account of which I have spoken, the Indians of the present day did not pretend to know anything about their origin. They were beyond the reach of all their traditions, and were lost in the abyss of unexplored antiquity.[8]

Ancient Sites of Habitation

In colonial times ancient sites of fortifications and occupation were found all over the hilltops of western New York. Everywhere abounded evidence that these lands had been occupied by prehistoric peoples who had been involved in war.

A Book of Mormon interpretation for this area is certainly consistent with that historical knowledge. Even in the centuries after the Nephites were gone, Lamanites or other peoples may have come into the area (Mormon 8:8, 9). Thus, this does not rule out the possibility that either Jaredites and/or Nephites may have previously occupied the same sites.

The noted historian E.G. Squire found:

> ...more than 1,000 sites in Ontario (Canandaigua), Livingston (Geneseo), Genesee (Batavia) and Monroe (Rochester) Counties. Nearly 500 sites chartered in Monroe County alone. In Genesee County are over 100 fortified hilltops and strongholds, and similar number of burial sites, and nearly 50 true mound...There is not an area of like size in the United States east of the Ohio and north of the Mason and Dixon Line where evidences of aboriginal occupation are so abundant.[9]

Those Remarkable Ruins, Again

It is reassuring to know that prolific ancient fortifications were discovered by early colonists who first came to proposed Book of Mormon lands in the area of western New York. While their observations are interesting and support a Book of Mormon interpretation, one must be very cautious in jumping to conclusions regarding these observations as external evidences that "prove" the Book of Mormon.

It is entirely possible that Lamanites following the destruction of the Nephites, carried on many Nephites practices, including the building of fortifications. Recall that following the last days of Cumorah, "the Lamanites are at war one with another...and no one knoweth the end of the war" (Mormon 8:8).

It is well known that the Iroquois, those peoples who occupied the lands of Map A at the coming of the Europeans, continually waged war on their enemies. Not only did they fight for conquest, but revenge was a significant factor (see Moroni 9:5, 23). This characteristic could have easily been carried on down for centuries since the days of the Nephites. Many of the ancient fortification sites of Map 6.1 may well have been due to the Iroquois, as some anthropologists suggest.

Another consideration is that other European peoples may also have penetrated and established isolated colonies in ancient North America. This may have been Celtic people, for which there are some evidences.[10] Or, this quite likely may have been Viking peoples, since their presence in ancient North America preceded Christopher Columbus by at least 500 years.[11]

Many of the descriptions of the ancient peoples who occupied ancient western New York involved large boned people of huge proportions. The Vikings fit such characteristics. The ancients also practiced the art of metal crafts with iron and copper, technologies skillfully practiced by the Vikings. The Vikings possibly brought horses to ancient America. Horse bones have been found in ancient burial mounds in eastern America, but they have been generally discredited as being fakes. Little on the subject is reported.

Any of these topics may be debatable. But the purpose here is merely to recognize that there are pitfalls involved when attempting to look to archaeological ruins or other evidences as external proofs for the Book of Mormon.

What a beautiful thought it is that it was within divine providence that enough of the ruins of the Jaredites and Nephites were allowed to remain for colonists to observe them, that their testimonies could inspire confidence and reassurance for modern readers who accept that Book of Mormon peoples once occupied the lands proposed in Map A.

Inasmuch as the archaeological picture has become quite muddy, potential evidences destroyed by the spade and the plow, in this way the Book of Mormon can speak to readers as "one crying from the dead, yea, even as one speaking out of the dust" (Moroni 10:27).

In Summary

This chapter has completed the identification of a most important feature of geography found in western New York, the "line" that separated Bountiful from Desolation, northward from Zarahemla. The consequence of this is that it brings Jaredite inhabitation much closer to the land of Zarahemla, into lands that lie below the narrow neck of land, and not far northward above the narrow neck as typically believed.

In the next chapter it will be logically demonstrated that the Jaredite ruins discovered by the Limhi expedition were not far from Zarahemla. Consequently this implies that the Hill Cumorah was not all that far from Zarahemla.

Surprisingly, this supports the idea that the Hill Cumorah of the Book of Mormon lay in lands found below the narrow neck of land, consistent with where it is found in western New York today.

Endnote
(see Bibliography for references)

1. Shetrone (1930).
2. McGavin and Bean (1949). Copies of this book may be hard to obtain. Delbert Curtis, in his book Christ in North America (Tigard: Resource Communications Inc., 1993), quotes verbatim several chapters taken from the work of McGavin and Bean.
3. Turner (23-26). Quotation by Curtis (1993, 183-184).
4. McIntosh (p.285). Cited by Curtis (1993, 184-185).
5. McGavin & Bean (1948, 19). See Curtis (1993, 191).
6. The following information was provided to me through a personal communication. Dr. Kenneth Tankersley, of State University of New York, at Brockport, lives close to Route 104, not far from the "Ridge Road," and is a professional archaeologist, with a specialty in Paleo-Indian field research. The information presented here is based upon opinions expressed by Dr. Tankersley, gleaned from a personal discussion with him. Archaeologists refer to this Escarpment ridge as "The Strand Line."

   Supposedly a few of the fortifications have been radiocarbon dated to an age of about 1,000 years. Such ages are seen to fit the time period of the early Iroquois Indians. However, the entire region about the ridge also contained sites, a few of which have been dated as Late Archaic. From a Book of Mormon interpretation, this period of time would be commensurate with possible Jaredite or Nephite occupation.

   Other information concerning the ancient fortifications on the Escarpment ridge was taken from State Archaeologist Beth Wellman, of the State Museum at Albany. A current study seems to show that those few New York sites identified as being Hopewell (Ohio Mound Builder culture) were incorrectly identified, and they are not Hopewell as some archaeologists had believed. This tends to displace New York from Ohio Mound Builder influences.
7. Found in Morrison's Annals of Western New York (1975), are a few references which support this idea. "A few settlers in each year until 1809, when the great natural thoroughfare, the Ridge Road, was opened, inducing a much more rapid influx of settlers. Immigrants continued to pour in rapidly and settle near the Ridge, until settlement was checked by the War of 1812...The Settlers generally choose locations in the immediate vicinity of Ridge Road, and continued to do so until the completion of the Erie Canal, when regions to the south began rapidly to fill up...the county has taken front rank among the best agricultural regions of the state."
8. McGavin & Bean (1948, 60). See Curtis (1993, 211-212).
9. McGavin & Bean (1948, 65). See Curtis (1993, 217-218).
10. McClone & Leonard (1986).
11. Mallory (1950).

Chapter 7

Limhi's Lost Expedition

KING LIMHI SENT AN EXPEDITION OUT FROM THE LAND
of Nephi to find the land of Zarahemla. This expedition became
lost, and discovered what they believed to be the land of Zarahemla.
Instead, the expedition had discovered Jaredite ruins and twenty-four
gold plates, the record of the Jaredites.

The significance of this expedition is that it clearly demonstrates
that Jaredite lands were not all that far from the land of Zarahemla.
Please notice from Map A that the Hill Cumorah is located approximately 30 miles northeast of the location proposed for the heart of
Zarahemla.

The purpose of this chapter is to demonstrate how logical it was for
the Limhi expedition to deduce that they had arrived at Zarahemla.
But the consequence is that Book of Mormon accounts support the
idea that the lands of Zarahemla were much closer to Hill Cumorah
than most Book of Mormon geographers recognize today.

Historically, it was an analysis of the Limhi expedition that convinced geographers that the setting for the Book of Mormon was

indeed a *local geography*.[1] Simply, this means that Book of Mormon events took place over distances measured only in hundreds of miles, rather than in thousands of miles as popularly believed in the early days of the Church.

This short chapter outlines, in some detail, accounts that clearly indicate that the Limhi expedition most likely took place in western New York. Features of geography peculiar to the area play a role in helping to understand the importance of this expedition in establishing that Jaredite lands lay south of the narrow neck of land, encompassing the Hill Cumorah.

The Discovery of Coriantumr

In the Book of Ether it is noted that the Jaredites were completely destroyed at or near Hill Cumorah (see Ether 15:12, 14, 23, 29). There were no survivors except "one Coriantumr," who was discovered by the people of Zarahemla (Omni 1:21).

Now if Coriantumr was a survivor of the total Jaredite destruction at Hill Ramah/Cumorah, this suggests that his discovery by Mulekites probably occurred in the near vicinity of Hill Cumorah, likely in Mulekite lands that encompassed the Hill Cumorah.

Please recall that in the Book of Ether it is mentioned that in an early period of the Jaredites, Omer departed out of his land, traveled many days, and passed by hill Ramah/Cumorah (Ether 9:3); he was joined by Nimrah later on (Ether 9:9). This certainly suggests that the Hill Ramah/Cumorah must have played some kind of a central role in Jaredite geography, from the very beginning of the Jaredites in America.

As pointed out in a previous chapter, because of the wickedness of the Jaredites, Jaredite lands became occupied by the Mulekites (see Ether 13:21). Now, since Jaredite lands included the Hill Cumorah, then lands of the peoples of Zarahemla (Mulekites) also included the Hill Cumorah.

Thus these considerations clearly are in support of the idea that Hill Cumorah was indeed in close proximity to the land of Zarahemla.

The Expedition

In the days of King Limhi, about 122 B.C., an expedition was sent out from the land of Nephi to search for the land of Zarahemla. Because Limhi and his people were in bondage to the Lamanites, King Limhi desired that he could make contact with his brethren in Zarahemla, in hopes that they might help to deliver his people from Lamanite bondage.

An expedition was sent out to find the land of Zarahemla, but they became lost in a land on the north, where they found remains of a previous civilization, namely that of the Jaredites.

The account of the Limhi expedition states that they found "bones" and "ruins of buildings," those that once belonged to the Jaredites. Thus the expedition missed its target at Zarahemla, overshot its mark and discovered lands previously occupied by the Jaredites. An important issue is, the over-shot distance was not all that much, in contrast to much greater distances typically proposed by other Book of Mormon geographers.

Please refer to Map 7.1 presented on page 77. This is a map which illustrates some significant journeys from and to the land of Zarahemla. While the paths are shown as straight lines, they more likely were zig-zag paths, perhaps much more torturous than shown, running through wilderness areas.

Expeditions to Zarahemla

In referring to Map 7.1, if travel had been through wilderness areas, heavily forested, with steep hilly terrain, people could have easily gotten disoriented and lost. Actual path distances could have easily been double the scale amounts.

These factors would enter into time of travel considerations.

Also illustrated on Map 7.1 is a portion of the proposed River Sidon, taken here as the Genesee River, where its highbank areas would have presented a rugged wilderness area to the Nephites. This feature of real geography was considered in devising Map 7.1.

Journey No. 1

King Limhi was the son of wicked King Noah, who was the son of Zeniff. It was Zeniff who had departed from Zarahemla with an "army" to reclaim the lands of their father's inheritance in the land of Nephi, but an internal fight occurred near the land of Nephi. Only 50 of his army remained, and they were forced to return to Zarahemla (Omni 1:28; Mosiah 9:2). It is quite likely that this army had a good idea of which way to go, in what direction the land of Nephi lay from Zarahemla.

Journey No. 2

Zeniff was successful on his second attempt and, with an unspecified number of people, did obtain possession of the land of Nephi, even though it was done so under the yoke of Lamanite oppression (Mosiah 9:10).

Journey No. 3

After Zeniff departed out of Zarahemla, three years later King Mosiah dispatched 16 strong men to go up to the land of Lehi-Nephi to make inquiry concerning those who had left. It took forty days of wandering in the wilderness to reach the land of Nephi.

Thus these three expeditions to the land of Nephi were made with a general knowledge of how to reach the land of Nephi.

Journey No. 4

It was only natural that King Limhi desired to know of his grandfather's people "down" in Zarahemla, and to tell their brethren of their plight with the Lamanites. Thus there was a desire to leave the land of Nephi and make contact with their brethren in the land of Zarahemla.

Going "down" to Zarahemla meant a journey from southern highlands, northward and down to Zarahemla.

Thus King Limhi "caused" that an expedition of forty-three of his people should take a journey into the wilderness that they might find

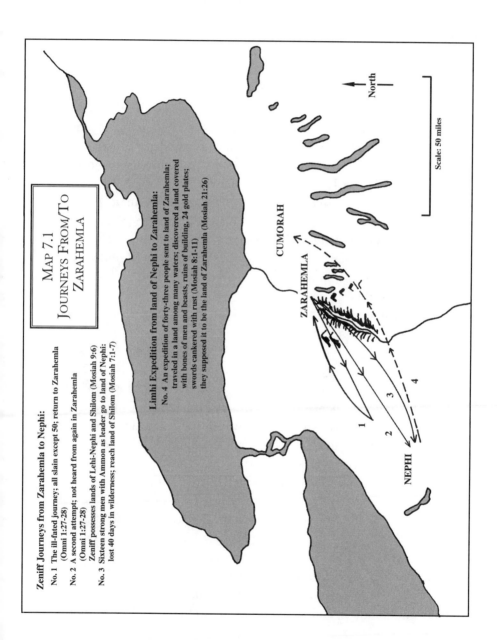

Zeniff Journeys from Zarahemla to Nephi:

No. 1 The ill-fated journey; all slain except 50; return to Zarahemla
(Omni 1:27-28)

No. 2 A second attempt; not heard from again in Zarahemla
(Omni 1:27-28)

Zeniff possesses lands of Lehi-Nephi and Shilom (Mosiah 9:6)

No. 3 Sixteen strong men with Ammon as leader go to land of Nephi:
lost 40 days in wilderness; reach land of Shilom (Mosiah 7:1-7)

Limhi Expedition from land of Nephi to Zarahemla:

No. 4 An expedition of forty-three people sent to land of Zarahemla;
traveled in a land among many waters; discovered a land covered
with bones of men and beasts, ruins of building, 24 gold plates;
swords cankered with rust (Mosiah 8:1-11)
they supposed it to be the land of Zarahemla (Mosiah 21:26)

MAP 7.1
JOURNEYS FROM/TO
ZARAHEMLA

CUMORAH

ZARAHEMLA

NEPHI

North

Scale: 50 miles

1

2

3

4

the land of Zarahemla where their brethren lived (Mosiah 8:7). Instead, the expedition became lost and discovered a land which had been peopled, and which was covered with "dry" bones.

Analysis of the Expedition

There are several significant things about this Limhi expedition to be considered. First, the Limhi expedition "traveled in a land among many waters" (Mosiah 8:8). Please notice from Map 7.1 how easy it would have been for this expedition to pass through a corridor between the Finger Lakes, a land of many waters.

Perhaps this occurred between lakes Keuka and Canandaigua, in the land of many waters (Map B). This path is suggested because it leads directly to the land of Hill Cumorah. Please notice just how easy the Limhi expedition could have missed their target at Zarahemla, in a wilderness setting among the tree covered high hills and deep valleys found in this region.

The people of the Limhi expedition had some idea of where Zarahemla was located in relation to the land of Nephi. Consequently, the expedition "supposed" that this land of ruins and bones was the land of Zarahemla (Mosiah 21:26).

Recall that Coriantumr and his people were destroyed at Hill Ramah/Cumorah, hence the vicinity of Hill Ramah/Cumorah was the most likely place where Ether would have left the twenty-four gold plates of Jaredite history, so that the Limhi expedition would eventually find them (Ether 15:33).

Since Coriantumr was discovered by the Mulekites, people of Zarahemla, it may be likely that Coriantumr had not wandered very far from Hill Ramah/Cumorah following the destruction of the Jaredites.

Recall that in the days of King Mosiah a large stone was brought to him containing the account of Coriantumr having been discovered by the people of Zarahemla, the Mulekites (Omni 1:20). This stone also gave a brief account about Coriantumr's fathers who had come out from the tower, and whose bones lay scattered in the land northward (Omni 1:22).

If this land "northward" was northward from Zarahemla, this would place this land northward directly in line with the site where

The Genesee River flows through a wilderness setting of Letchworth State Park, that lies along a line of sight between the proposed lands of Nephi and Zarahemla.

Northern Keuka Lake at Penn Yan. The land corridor between lakes Keuka and Canandaigua leads to Hill Cumorah in the north.

Hill Cumorah is located today, relative to the location proposed for Zarahemla in ancient New York (see Map A).

Thus it seems quite likely that the Limhi expedition did have some knowledge concerning the location of the land of Zarahemla, relative to the land of Nephi. After all, Zarahemla was the land of King Limhi's grandfather, Zeniff (Mosiah 7:9), and surely some kind of instructions must have been given on how to find Zarahemla, by people who had been there.

Thus when the Limhi expedition reached the land of the former Jaredites, there they discovered twenty-four gold plates left by Ether (Ether 15:33), and they *"supposed* it to be the land of Zarahemla" (Mosiah 21: 26).

It is likely that they were quite sure they had been to Zarahemla, because they returned to the land of Nephi having found nothing but dried bones in what they thought was Zarahemla.

As a testimony that they spoke the truth, they brought twenty-four plates filled with engravings, breastplates, and rusted swords without hilts, perhaps as evidence that they had been to Zarahemla (Mosiah 8:9–11).

In Summary

Now, from all the above considerations, it does not seem reasonable that the Limhi expedition would have missed their mark, the land of Zarahemla, by a huge distance factor as is typically thought.

In Journey No. 3 above, it took sixteen strong men forty days of wandering to travel from the land of Zarahemla, to the land of Nephi. According to Map A, this might have involved a "crow flight" distance of something like 110 miles.[2]

Thus when the Limhi expedition overshot the land of Zarahemla, and ended up near or at Hill Cumorah, this might have meant an overshoot of about twenty-five miles. This distance is quite reasonable and seems consistent with the idea that the land of Zarahemla was not located very far from Hill Cumorah, and it was located *below* the narrow neck of land.

A view of the Genesee River near Belfast.
This area may be a good candidate for lands lying
in what may have been the land of Judea.

A view of the Genesee River Valley seen from Route 63, northwest from Geneseo.
These fertile valley lands were most likely part of the land of Zarahemla.

Endnote
(see Bibliography for references)

1. F.A.R.M.S. (Sper, 1963).
2. In the popular Central American settings, the distances proposed between the lands of Nephi and Zarahemla range from 100 to 200 miles approximately. However, the Hill Cumorah is typically assumed to have been located in southern Mexico, in Veracruz. This leads to distances from the proposed lands of Zarahemla to the assumed Hill Cumorah as being approximately 200 miles. Thus for Central American settings, the Limhi expedition would have missed their mark by a huge overshoot factor of 200 miles. While such a large overshoot is possible, it seems unlikely. However, when one interprets the Limhi expedition according to Figure 7.1, the distance factors take on very realistic proportions.

   So why is the proposed Hill Cumorah chosen? First, the coastal lagoon waters of Veracruz are seen as a land of "many waters." Also the archaeological evidences for the ancient Olmec are found in this area, with the assumption that the Olmec were the Jaredites. In and of themselves, these are relatively weak arguments to support the existence of a second Hill Cumorah in Central America.

   It is ironical that an analysis of the Limhi expedition was a factor in helping geographers see that Book of Mormon events took place within a "local geography." Had that local geography been recognized as being centered around Hill Cumorah in western New York, there never would have arisen a need for a second Hill Cumorah.

Chapter 8

Destroyed by Spade & Plow

ONE MAY THINK THAT THE NEPHITES WERE A VERY numerous people, building large cities of impressive stone struc- tures. But the Book of Mormon can paint a completely different pic- ture. The Nephites were a people who lived in a vast wilderness area, built cities made of wood, and struggled against vast hostile Lamanite populations that inhabited the wilderness areas.

Why Such Large Numbers?

One might wonder how it came about that the Lamanites became so numerous so quick. First of all, the Lamanites were a migratory "blood-thirsty" people, "dwelling in tents, and wandering about in the wilderness" (Enos 1:20). When the Nephites joined the people of Zarahemla, described as being "exceedingly numerous," combined they were "not half so numerous as were the Lamanites" (Omni 1:17, Mosiah 25:3).

From an analysis of Book of Mormon accounts that mention the movements of the Lamanites, it appears that Nephite battles with the

Lamanites involved huge numbers of Lamanites, probably armies made up of almost the entire Lamanite warrior population of all the land, coming from many miles away to join in the battles against the Nephites.

If there was to be a battle, every blood-thirsty Lamanite wanted to be included in the action. In this way, huge Lamanite armies were quickly assembled, moving quickly on foot over the entire geographic region of Book of Mormon lands. The less mobile Nephites, city dwellers and protectors of their cities, thus had much smaller populations than the numerous roving Lamanite hordes.

Small Nephite Populations

The following account might give some insight into what the size of Nephite populations may have been.

In about 125 B.C., King Benjamin caused that his people bring their tents and families and pitch them "round about the temple," with doors facing the temple, "that they might remain within their tents" and hear his words "within the walls of the temple." The turnout was so great that King Benjamin had to cause a tower to be erected, but even then their numbers were so great that his message had to be read to the multitude (Mosiah 2:1–8).

What might this mean? The significant thing is that even King Benjamin knew that his voice could only be heard so far, especially within a tent camp-out. If the temple walls were as huge as a square football field, probably less than 1,000 family tents could be jammed in.

But who could hear the human voice, even for these distances? Assuming an average family of seven, and that King Benjamin's estimate was off by a factor of three, this could mean that all the people of the land of Zarahemla probably numbered less than 20,000, and likely only half as much. This is not a large population for all the land of Zarahemla.

Lamanites and Indians

So where did the numerous Lamanites come from? How could these hunters of the forrest multiply so rapidly, as compared to the more civilized Nephites who practiced the arts of agriculture?

The answer may be that the descendants of Laman and Lemuel, starting from the very beginning, began to intermarry with other peoples who may have occupied neighboring lands. These people could have been the ancestors of those whom we know today as the Indians.

The idea is not far fetched.[1] This could explain why it is that the Lamanites adopted characteristics so similar to those of the Indians. Lamanite physical characteristics, through intermarriage, became like those of the Indians. The Lamanites adopted their manner of dress and adornment, their methods of warfare, and many other characteristics of the Indians. The Lamanites, through their idleness, abandoned their more civilized heritage, and adopted the ways of the Indians.

The large numbers of Lamanites would occur when the Lamanites joined with the numerous Indian peoples whose ranks they became part of.

Critics of the Book of Mormon have questioned how it is that so many diverse Indian tribes could have all descended from a single group, the Lamanites, in such a short time period.[2] In this proposed scenario, the Lamanites are seen as joining Indian tribes from neighboring lands. In this way the Lamanites became ancestors to certain North American Indian tribes, some of whom the Prophet Joseph Smith identified.[3]

Out Numbered Nephites

Within the first century B.C., "tens of thousands of the Lamanites were slain," and "the bodies of many thousands are moldering in heaps upon the face of the earth" (Alma 28:2, 11). How many Nephite warriors caused this destruction? Probably far, far fewer than the number of Lamanites killed. Why? Because the Nephites had the ability that a mere "fifty" could stand "against thousands" (Mosiah 11:19). Perhaps use of steel swords and some form of armor made this possible.

These considerations might mean that we need to revise our expectations on what to expect for a setting that is found in the Great Lakes area, which according to the archaeological record, always has been mostly a wilderness area. The Book of Mormon repeatedly refers to only a natural wilderness environment that surrounded the Nephite civilization.

Placing the Nephites and Lamanites in a Great Lakes setting for the Book of Mormon is much less of a challenge than it is for anywhere else in the world. What may be surprising to some is that the archaeological record of the area can be interpreted to be even more favorable to Book of Mormon interpretations than imagined. That this might be the case will be briefly explained next.

Expectations in New York

The Archaeology of New York State, a classic 1965 work by William Ritchie, is an important archaeological work on New York.[4] Yet his findings on the archaeological picture of western New York seem to be devoid of the kind of picture that one might think the Book of Mormon had painted, and seems to ignore the findings of the many historians who had recorded the discoveries of ancient earthworks, fortifications, and archaeological evidences discovered in western New York by its earliest observers.

The archeological record of the New York area seems quite misleading when one looks at sites that have been radiocarbon dated. Ritchie's sample collections show a huge gap in time, wherein there is practically no data. Surprisingly, almost nothing is dated within the time period 500 BC to AD 400, the period of the Nephites.

Noticing this can lead one to think that western New York never had a Nephite population. It would be easy to fail to understand why this is misleading, and to not comprehend the significance in this. Only after much research on the matter did this gap in archaeological knowledge become clear.

It seems obvious that the great bulk of the archaeological sites, covering the time period of the Nephites, were destroyed by the spade and the plow of the early colonists. Also, those few sites that remain are unacceptable for study because they were pilfered and badly damaged. The sites had been ravaged by people who destroyed most of what they found and often made errors in describing and interpreting their findings.

Many of the artifacts discovered were either pilfered, destroyed or lost. Then too, in some cases forgeries were involved, and unless the artifacts were discovered undisturbed in their original locations by competent professionals, the findings were considered difficult to interpret.

Advancing "civilization" has produced devastating effects on the archaeological record of western New York. Towns were built over former sites, farmers plowed over earthworks, digging up skulls and artifacts by the bushel basketful, and treasure hunters pilfered and destroyed most of the archaeological sites.

McGavin and Bean, in their 1948 book on *The Geography of the Book of Mormon*, report that many ancient grave sites were within the Book of Mormon lands proposed in this book.[5] It turns out that almost all of those wonderful ruins were destroyed, or rendered useless. While this may be sad, it seems consistent with what one might expect.

What Was Found?

The 1894 work of Cyrus Thomas, as presented in his *Mound Explorations*, is well known.[6] It is important to pay particular attention to his sections on New York. Therein Thomas gave his report on many of the "Indian" sites presented in Map 6.1. Thomas described many of the sites according to their design, and reported what the archaeological contents were, for those that remained in existence. He also identified many sites, of which very little or nothing remained by the time he examined them.

The following is a brief summary of some of Thomas' interesting findings.

Burial mounds, earthworks and fortifications were found over the entire area that is here identified as Book of Mormon lands. Found were bone pits, fish pond traps, and weirs, etc., where many were found in the Finger Lakes area.

Graves typically contained items such as copper beads, fragments of copper ornaments, scraps of mica, clay pipes, stone pipes, long knife-like spear heads, stone gorgets, pieces of iron, arrowheads, celts, chisels, concave disks, mortars and pestles.

Many of the sites were found in the area of Lake Chautauqua. It is known that the French occupied many of the Indian lands of this area, thus mixing artifacts and leading to a possible confusion as to who the people were that were buried in these apparently ancient graves.

Thomas pointed out that later generation Indians were known to use the same burial sites as their ancestors. Thus without the original undisturbed burial sites available, much confusion resulted over what was found.

Circular and elliptical earthen enclosures were discovered that were from 1.5 to 3 acres in area. Enclosures were formed by piling up the earth, creating walls that in some cases supported timbers. Some enclosures were only twenty feet in diameter, while others were as much as sixty feet in diameter. These were apparently works of defense, situated on tops of hills, sometimes overlooking a bluff, or between two valleys.

Undoubtedly some of the ancient fortifications, palisaded forts, were the work of Iroquois Indians of later generations. A few sites were dated to times after A.D. 1000. Yet many of the fortification sites were naturally occurring and very likely they had been used for untold generations. Who knows, based upon perishable building materials, how many generations of people had used these same naturally occurring sites of fortification?

Found were skeletons sometimes buried in rows, and sometimes in tiers, covered by earth between layers. Sometimes skeletons were found seated in a circle, back to back, feet outward. Sometimes skeletons were seated, facing to the east. Sometimes food had been placed in jars with the skeleton, possibly indicating a belief in a life after death. In most of the cases the skeletons either turned to dust when touched, or were badly decayed. No radiocarbon dating methods were available to these early archaeologists.

It was discovered that the Indians dug one foot deep trenches in which timbers were placed vertical, about 2.5 feet apart, to form a stockade or palisade. Dirt was then placed in the trench between the timbers. An otherwise flimsy structure was strengthened by side braces. However, one can easily see that when the structure was destroyed, no pole holes were left behind in the ground. The structures simply toppled over, and the timbers were left on top of the ground to rot. Thus no wood remained behind that might have been used in radiocarbon dating.

Of particular interest might be the Escarpment area east of Niagara Falls. Bone pits were found not far from the Niagara River, that contained skeletons of both sexes, thrown in without order. One was found in which sixty skulls were brought to the surface. Some pits contained many hundred of skeletons. No bullet holes were found in the skulls. Some of these bone pits may have contained skeletons where the flesh was removed from the deceased, perhaps in ceremony, thus creating a mass burial site, either all at once, or over time.

Emerging from details presented by Thomas, that are too numerous to present here, is a picture that many of the archaeological sites had been destroyed by the 1880s. Thomas gleaned much of his information from what he was told by local residents as well as from that found in written accounts. His report includes some three dozen specific sites that he considered worthy of mention, while he alludes to many other destroyed sites.

The archaeological discoveries in New York are not particularly peculiar to the area. Mounds and fortification sites were found all over the eastern United States and Canada. Their dates indicate that when Book of Mormon peoples came to America, they may have adopted features of culture possessed by other peoples of whom they came into contact with over the 1,000 years of Nephite history. Contact may have occurred through wars or by peaceful trading outside of homelands.

It might now be seen why Ritchie's data seems so bleak for Book of Mormon interpretations. The archaeological records for time periods covered by the Book of Mormon in the proposed New York setting were basically destroyed. Neither Ritchie nor other scholars did not consider them because the sites had been damaged, from a professional point of view.

It appears that when both the Jaredites and the Nephites came to lands set aside for them by the Lord, they found an empty Promised Land, not occupied by other nations. After the demise of the Nephites, these lands remained hidden from the world until the coming of the Colonists. The scant archaeological record seems in keeping with the ways of the Lord that our testimony of the Book of Mormon remain a matter of faith, and not based upon external proofs found from archaeology.

The Adena and the Hopewell

Whether the Nephites or Lamanites influenced, or were influenced by either the Adena or Hopewell cultures of Ohio can only be conjectured. Adena mound building characteristics began as early as 1000 B.C., and started to be phased out around 200 B.C. by the merger of Hopewellian influences.[7] This time frame seems to match a Nephite presence in America. Also, in the last couple of centuries B.C., Nephite culture began to grow enormously. Is it possible that some Hopewellian influences affected them?

The Hopewellian burial practices became mound building on a grandiose scale becoming more elaborate with bigger and more majestic mounds. Hopewellian culture has also been found in Illinois, wherein evidences indicate that vast trade and cultural exchange networks had existed, reaching far and wide.[8]

By A.D. 100 Hopewellian culture dominated. At about A.D. 400 the Hopewell culture began to decline. Could it have been influenced by the emergence of a new victorious Lamanite people who then became involved in wars among themselves, perhaps over the spoils of war, following the last of the Nephites at Hill Cumorah in A.D. 380? The reason for the decline of Hopewell culture is unknown. One theory is that "raiding rather than exchange became a viable way of obtaining access to more resources."[9]

Some archaeologist today question whether there ever were any Hopewellian influences found in New York sites. Apparently a new interpretation suggests that some Late Archaic sites have been mistakenly identified as Hopewellian.[10]

The Book of Mormon makes no mention of trade with other peoples. It appears that the focus of Nephite attention was warring with the Lamanites. Yet such a possibility for trade cannot be ruled out. It is possible that Book of Mormon peoples traded with peoples from the Ohio Valley because some artifacts found in New York mounds seem to be comparable to that of the Ohio Adena, although the evidence is only scant.

The fact that the Allegheny river originates in New York, runs south to Pittsburgh, Pennsylvania, where it joins the Monongahela River to form the Ohio River, suggests that some cultural exchange must surely have occurred with the peoples of Ohio, over the approximately 1,000 years of Nephite civilization in New York and Canada.

The Algonquian and Iroquois

The Indians who lived along the borders of the Atlantic coast, from North Carolina to Nova Scotia, were designated as Algonquian. Further to the west were the Iroquois, who spoke a different language altogether.

The Iroquois occupied those lands specifically identified in Map A (front cover). The Iroquois found other Algonquian peoples to the north and west, and to the south in Pennsylvania, whose language they could not speak.[11]

Today the origins of the Algonquian peoples are still unknown. However, their form of language dates into prehistoric times. Scholars now believe that the Iroquois have always inhabited their historic lands. They did not come from the Southeast, nor did they migrate from the West, as originally believed. Today opinions favor an origin dating from the Late Archaic period.

As Seen Today

The early colonists in western New York literally destroyed one of the greatest archaeological treasures within the United States. Nowhere else in the country was such an abundance of ancient fortification sites and burial mounds to be found. However, in the agricultural pursuits of the colonists, the plough literally destroyed evidence for earthworks and fortified cities.

Placing the setting for the Book of Mormon in the area of western New York, southern Ontario, Canada, and portions of Pennsylvania and Ohio, presents a new sort of challenge. However, the challenge can be met. It seems that a Book of Mormon setting located in the western New York area can stand on its own merits, perhaps more there than anywhere else on earth.

Endnote
(see Bibliography for references)

1. The ancient Israelites sometimes had problems with their people intermarrying with the Gentiles.
2. Roberts (1985, 36). "Philogic studies have divided the Indian languages into five distinct linguistic stocks which show very little relationship. It does not appear that this diversity in the nature and grammatical constructions of Indian tongues could obtain if the Indians were descendants of a people who possessed as highly developed a language as the ancient Hebrew, but indicates that the division of the Indians into separate stocks occurred long before their language was developed beyond the most primitive kind of articulations. Again, the time allowed from the landing of Lehi is much too short to account for the observed diversity."
3. Joseph Smith (1978, vol.4, 401). Indian tribes that the Prophet identified had all moved westward from their original tribal lands, located in eastern North America.
4. Ritchie (1965).
5. McGavin and Bean (1948).
6. Cyrus Thomas (1985).
7. Dragoo (1966, Introduction).
8. Fagan (1991, 375).
9. Fagan (1991, 383).
10. This information was obtained from by New York State Archaeologist Beth Wellman, New York State Museum at Albany, March 31, 1995.
11. Beauchamp (1968).

Chapter 9

Where the Nephites Lived

O NE CAN LOOK AT A MAP OF THE GREAT LAKES AND notice the existence of a small narrow neck of land at Niagara. The proximity of this narrow neck of land near Palmyra, not far from where the Hill Cumorah is located, is convincing evidence that Book of Mormon lands may lie somewhere in this vicinity.

The Genesee River flows quietly under interstate I-90, hardly noticed by the casual traveler. Yet this river very well matches Book of Mormon requirements for the River Sidon. Knowledge of this river, so close to the Hill Cumorah, further adds to the proposition that it had something to do with Book of Mormon times.

Through the distraction of the deafening roar and mist of Niagara Falls, few people realize that the Niagara River is a "place," by the narrow neck of land, where water from a sea "divides the land." Yet according to the Book of Ether, this historic place was quite likely well known to the Jaredites. Knowledge of this important "place" gives added assurance that it played a role in Book of Mormon geography.

The Niagara Falls are mighty, as all tourists recognize, but students of the Book of Mormon have not recognized them as the "waters of Ripliancum." Their presence, not far from Hill Cumorah represents one more piece of evidence that suggests Book of Mormon events did take place in these lands.

As travelers today make their way along the Escarpment Ridge on Route 104, there are probably none that would realize that this ridge was once heavily fortified by an ancient people, a people who mysteriously disappeared into oblivion through wars of extermination. Yet Book of Mormon accounts are convincing that this indeed happened in this area.

These correspondences in Book of Mormon geography are striking indeed. Taken collectively, in light of their proximity to Hill Cumorah, one can only ask, where else on earth is it likely that Book of Mormon events took place?

In this chapter and those that follow, it will be assumed that the likely geographic setting for the Book of Mormon is to be found in the area of western New York.

Map A was composed with these key features of geography in mind. They are fundamentally important, and as such, form the basis for this Map. From such a basis, it now becomes possible to determine, with some degree of assurance, where Nephite cities and lands may have been located. How this can be accomplished will unfold in this and in the chapters to follow.

Needless to say, the process is complicated. Yet by using clues found in Book of Mormon accounts, the task can be reasonably accomplished.

A Major Clue

Over a period of decades, students have attempted to locate cities and lands spoken of in the Book of Mormon based upon their internal consistency of one with another. The maps produced are referred to as "internal geographies." Illustrated in Appendix A are several such internal geography maps.

Other geographers have attempted to place cities and lands in a real-world geographic setting. Typically such attempts have been focused around lands found in the Central Americas. Proposed Maps for this area can also be found in Appendix A.[1]

Placing Book of Mormon lands in the area of western New York has a singular distinction. As has been demonstrated thus far in this book, key features of Book of Mormon geography match those found in the area.

Thus one can proceed on the assumption that this match is not a mere coincidence, with some degree of assurance that the match is quite genuine. However, the task of matching further Book of Mormon correspondences to the New York geography is far from a simple matter.

As it turns out, a major clue is found in a map of former Indian settlements in western New York (Cornell University Map Room). This map was produced by Frank E. Richards and is dated 1957. After noting areas of sparse habitation, these are outlined as wilderness areas on the Richards map and is presented on page 97, as Map 9.1.

As such, the Richards map indicates where pre-historic peoples lived and suggests their wilderness environment.

In the Richards map, some of the village sites were designated as being *unfortified*, some were protected by *earthworks*, and some were fortified by *stockades*.

A slight revision of Richards' map was published in 1968, and it can be found in Thompson's *Geography of New York*.[2] However, Map 9.1 represents a modification of the Richards map, where areas of low population density are outlined as wilderness areas. The reason for this is as follows.

Book of Mormon accounts relate that the Nephites built *earthworks*, in that they dug ditches and formed high banks (Alma 49:4, 18, 22). The Nephites also built frameworks of pickets on top of the ridges of earth, thus forming *stockades* (Alma 50:1–4). Thus the Richards map of village sites contains some clues where the Nephites may have lived. Seen as Indian (Lamanite) sites, it is possible that the Nephites occupied these same desirable locations, centuries earlier.

It is reasonable that the pre-historic peoples who occupied the village sites of Map 9.1 lived in the more desirable areas. Notice that these areas are typically near rivers or bodies of water. By outlining areas of sparse habitation, through Map 9.1, one can get a good idea of where wilderness areas most likely existed in Nephite times. That these assumptions can be justified will be investigated.

Thus Map 9.1 might provide a clue, a starting point, from which to begin. While the Lamanites typically lived in wilderness areas, living as hunters, over long periods of Nephite history, they fought against the Nephites and took possession of their cities. Thus not all Lamanite peoples lived only as hunters in the wilderness, they also occupied cities.

In the discussion that follows, please refer to Map 9.1 and note the correspondences with that proposed in Map A.

Zarahemla: Center of the Land

Please notice that Map 9.1 indicates a relatively dense occupation of lands near the northern reaches of the Genesee River. Such a high density of fortified villages in this area suggests the desirability of these lands, those immediately north of the western Finger Lakes, making them a good candidate for the land of Zarahemla.

Lamanites who marched down to the land of Zarahemla, "durst not come into the heart of their [Nephite] lands to attack that great city Zarahemla, which lay "in the center of the land." Please note Helaman 1:17–27 uses the phrase "center of the land" three times. For this reason Map A indicates the location of the city of Zarahemla in the center of the land, in what may have been the heart of Nephite lands.

The Land of Nephi

From Map 9.1, an area of dense occupation can also be seen in the area east of Lake Chautauqua, which in turn lies slightly north and west of the head of the Genesee River. This area seems to be a good candidate for the *heart* of the land of Nephi. Book of Mormon accounts suggest such a location, relative to the head of Sidon, lying in the southwest quarter of the land.

Other accounts suggest that the land of Nephi was an extensive land, often mostly occupied by the Lamanites. The River Sidon most likely acted as a "line" of demarkation, separating "Nephites and Lamanites, between the land of Zarahemla and the land of Nephi" (Alma 50:11). This is reasonable because "the land of Nephi did run

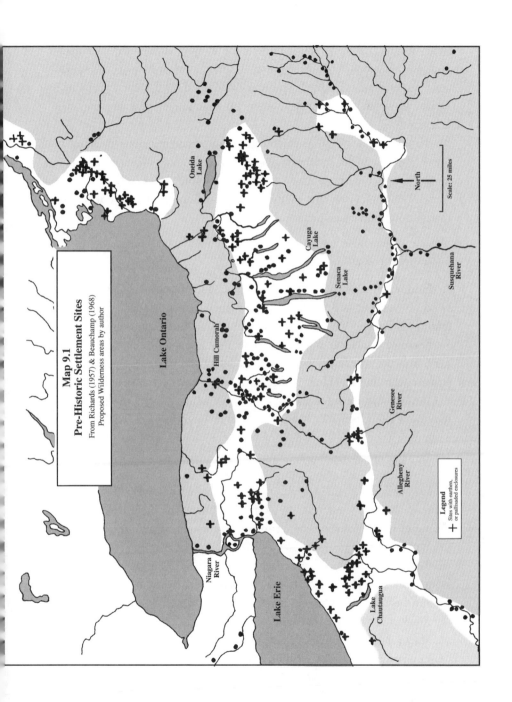

Map 9.1
Pre-Historic Settlement Sites
From Richards (1957) & Beauchamp (1968)
Proposed Wilderness areas by author

Lake Ontario

Oneida Lake

Cayuga Lake

Senaca Lake

Susquehana River

Hill Cumorah

Genesee River

Allegheny River

Niagara River

Lake Erie

Lake Chautauqua

North

Scale: 25 miles

Legend
+ Sites with earthen, or palisaded enclosures

in a straight course from the east to the west" (Alma 50:8). For these and other reasons, Map A suggests that the land of Nephi was southwest of the River Sidon. It spanned westward, along the shores of a west sea, south, (Lake Erie), from an east sea on the north (Lake Ontario).

Almost all Book of Mormon geographers agree that the land of Nephi was near the southern reaches of the River Sidon. Some place it in the southwest quarter of the land, while others place it more directly south. Thus the position suggested in Map A is entirely in conformity with most proposals.

Cities in the East

Notice from Map 9.1 that in close association with Cayuga lake were several fortified villages. Also further east, just south of Oneida lake is an even greater concentration of fortified villages.

Book of Mormon accounts relate that the Nephites were to "go forth into the east wilderness, even to the borders by the seashore, and possess the land." Here they built the cities of Moroni, Aaron, Nephihah, and Lehi (Alma 50:9–15). Just where these cites in the east may have been located will be a topic of discussion in the next chapter.

Wilderness Areas

Map 9.1 indicates a general wilderness area to the west of the Genesee River. Please refer to Map A and note the distances between the heart of the land of Nephi in the southwest, in relation to where the land of Zarahemla is placed on this map. In Alma 27:14 it is stated that a wilderness "divided the land of Nephi from the land of Zarahemala." When Gideon and his party journeyed from Shilom in the land of Nephi, "after many days in the wilderness they arrived in the land of Zarahemla (Mosiah 22:13).

Map 9.1 suggests a wilderness area east of Cayuga Lake. This can be seen to be consistent with an "east wilderness," to the "borders by the seashore," mentioned in Alma 50:9.

Map 9.1 suggests that the southern reaches of the Genesee River were also a wilderness area. This is in agreement with Alma 43:22, where a wilderness is mentioned in association with the head of the River Sidon (Alma 43:22).

While these matters give us some feeling for the outer perimeters associated with an assumed "local geography," there is no reason to exclude lands reaching much further from this area. However, one might note that the Book of Mormon is really only a very abbreviated account, and surely Book of Mormon lands must have extended much further than those proposed in Map A.[3]

Anciently Occupied

One should not expect that the sites of Map 9.1 represent a detailed picture of Nephite city locations. Perhaps later generations of Lamanites occupied these sites in recent centuries. Yet, it is reasonable that these same sites could have also been occupied by Book of Mormon peoples in ancient times.

It is the general pattern of occupation suggested by this map that can be useful in considering the likely correspondence between Nephite settlement patterns and the geography of western New York.

The geographic features of Map A, combined with wilderness areas suggested in map 9.1, are presented as Map 9.2, seen on page 102. Please refer to this map as interpretations are made relative to the book of Alma.

Correspondences with Alma 22

King Lamoni's father was king over all of the land. Alma 22 is a description of the land wherein this king's people lived. Thus in describing the lands his people occupied, this king's account gives a rather good description of what may have been lands occupied by the Nephites in western New York.

Please consider carefully the following verses taken from Alma 22, with key points of geographic interpretation indicated in italics. Correspondences with Map 9.2 can be noted. Some points of emphasis, as well as added comments, are presented in italics. Numbered references are interpreted on Map 9.2.

View from "Dayaitgao," site of a former Seneca village, near Mt. Morris.
Lands on the right may have been in the land of Zarahemla.

The valley lying east of Randolph on route 241.
These lands may have been part of the lands lying in the heart of the land of Nephi.

VERSE 27:

(1) His people [Lamanites] were in all his land, "in all the regions *round about*, which was bordering even to the sea, on the *east* and on the *west*,"

(lands through wilderness regions from one end of the sea on the north, round about the bordering southern wilderness to the other end of the northern sea. This singular sea mentioned is taken as Lake Ontario)

(2) "and which [*sea*] was divided from the land of Zarahemla by a [Bountiful] *narrow strip of wilderness*, which ran from the *sea east* even to the *sea west*,"

(Note that it was "the narrow strip of wilderness" that divided the sea on the north from the land of Zarahemla. This strip of wilderness ran through borderlands just south of the sea, from the eastern end of the sea (Lake Ontario), to the western end of the same sea. This peculiar description appears to be unique to the proposed New York geography)[4]

(2) "and [his people were] *round about* on the borders of the seashore [on the west] and the borders of the *wilderness* [Bountiful] which was on the *north* by the land of Zarahemla,

(3) through the borders of *Manti*, by the *head* of the *River Sidon*, running from the *east* towards the *west*, and thus were the Lamanites and the Nephites divided."

VERSE 28:

(4) The more idle part of the Lamanites were "through the *wilderness* which was on the *west*, in the land of Nephi; yea, and also on the *west* of the land of Zarahemla, in the borders by the *seashore,* and on the *west* in the land of Nephi, in the place of their fathers' first inheritance, thus bordering along by the *seashore*."

(this seems consistent with the land of Nephi lying west of the River Sidon, as indicated on Map A)

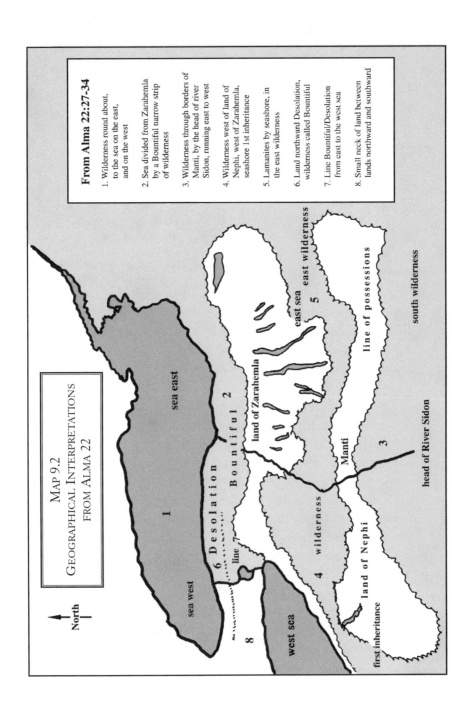

MAP 9.2
GEOGRAPHICAL INTERPRETATIONS
FROM ALMA 22

North

From Alma 22:27-34

1. Wilderness round about, to the sea on the east, and on the west

2. Sea divided from Zarahemla by a Bountiful narrow strip of wilderness

3. Wilderness through borders of Manti, by the head of river Sidon, running east to west

4. Wilderness west of land of Nephi, west of Zarahemla, seashore 1st inheritance

5. Lamanites by seashore, in the east wilderness

6. Land northward Desolation, wilderness called Bountiful

7. Line Bountiful/Desolation from east to the west sea

8. Small neck of land between lands northward and southward

sea east

sea west

west sea

Desolation

Bountiful

land of Zarahemla

line 7

8

first inheritance

wilderness

land of Nephi

Manti

head of River Sidon

east sea

east wilderness

line of possessions

south wilderness

1

2

3

4

5

6

VERSE 29:

(5) "...many Lamanites [were] on the *east* by the *seashore*," whither the Nephites had driven them. And thus the Nephites were nearly surrounded by the Lamanites."

(The most reasonable interpretation for an "east sea" is Cayuga Lake for reasons that will be explained later)

(3) "Nephites had taken possession of all the northern parts of the land bordering on the [south] *wilderness*, at the *head* of the River Sidon, from the *east* to the *west, round about* on the *wilderness* side;

(Note how well the cardinal directions of north, south, east and west apply to Map A)

(2) [Nephites were] on the *north*, even until they came to the land which they called *Bountiful*."

(Recall that Bountiful was a wilderness)

VERSE 30:

(6) "It [Bountiful] *bordered* upon the land which they called *Desolation*, it being so far *northward* that it came into the land...which was discovered by the people of Zarahemla...the place of their first landing."

(Notice how well this description of Desolation fits, being northward from Zarahemla, and yet not above the narrow neck of land)

VERSE 31:

(2) "Thus the land on the *northward* was called *Desolation*, and the land on the *southward* was called Bountiful...it being the *wilderness*..."

(Northward and southward are not directions in reference to the narrow neck of land)

VERSE 32:

(7) "It was only the distance of a day and a half journey for a Nephite, on the *line* Bountiful and the land

Desolation, from the *east* to the *west sea*; and thus the land of Nephi and the land of Zarahemla were *nearly surrounded by water,"*

(Recall from previous discussions, that the "line" ran from the east, to a west sea extension of Lake Ontario; also note how well the proposed lands of Nephi and Zarahemla are surrounded by water; rivers, lakes, and seas)

(8) "there being a *small neck of land* between the *land northward* and the *land southward."*

(it is here that one must distinguish between lands northward and southward relative to the small neck, in contrast with lands northward and southward relative to Zarahemla)

VERSE 33:
(2) Nephites inhabited "...the land *Bountiful*...from the *east* to the *west sea*..."

(Notice that the Bountiful wilderness extended from the east, to a west extension of the same body of water, identified as Lake Ontario)

VERSE 34:
"Thus the Lamanites could have no more possessions only in the land of Nephi, and the wilderness round about."

Now, the correspondences between these Book of Alma accounts and the areas presented in Map 9.2 can be seen as striking indeed.

Cities and Lands of Map A

In locating cities and lands found on Map A, these accounts found in Alma 22 were considered, taking into account the real-world geography found in the area of western New York. However, practically all other Book of Mormon descriptions of geography were also carefully considered, and analyzed in the context of Map A. In this way consistency with all Book of Mormon accounts was sought.

Interlocking the association of all cities and lands mentioned in the Book of Mormon is like solving a very complex puzzle. It is complicated because many of the pieces are not clearly outlined, nor are we always given a clear account of their relationship to the other pieces of the puzzle. In the next chapter, some interesting and challenging pieces of the puzzle will be considered.

Endnote
(see Bibliography for references)

1. F.A.R.M.S (1990). John Sorenson has compiled a source book that tabulates and provides information on maps of Book of Mormon geography, historically proposed. His extensive research into the matter helps one to obtain a feel for the extensive attempts that have gone into trying to decipher the geographic setting for the Book of Mormon. Sorenson tabulates information, by author, on some 68 attempts to locate the geography of the Book of Mormon, with accompanying maps in many cases.
2. Thompson (1966).
3. Research on the matter reveals that there are other maps that extend Indian occupation sites beyond southwestern New York, on into Ohio and Pennsylvania. Some of these sites were a consideration in attempting to locate the land of Nephi. It appears that the land of Nephi extended further south from the area of Lake Chautauqua, down the Allegheny River, for some distance. However, Map A only proposes an approximate boundary for this and other lands mentioned in the Book of Mormon.
4. As can be seen from the maps of Appendix A, geographers typically interpret this account as involving two seas, rather than one. It is assumed that the narrow strip of wilderness spanned from a sea on the west, to another sea on the east. Such an interpretation might seem possible in Map A of this book, involving Lake Erie (sea on west) and Lake Cayuga (sea on the east). The problem with this is that the narrow strip of wilderness would not divide the sea(s) from the land of Zarahemla, as the account mentions. This same problem exists for the other maps of Appendix A.

Chapter 10

Puzzling Nephite Cities and Lands

.

HOW CAN ONE BEGIN TO DETERMINE THE APPROXIMATE whereabouts of cities and lands mentioned in the Book of Mormon? It only makes sense that one needs to begin the quest by starting out in the correct geographic area in the first place. Otherwise one could not hope to expect to achieve any degree of success or assurance.

The locations for cities and lands given in Map A have a degree of uncertainty, and they were probably located only in the vicinity of where they are shown. Beginning with Hill Cumorah, a known point of geography in western New York, we have sought to establish a proper narrow neck of land, a proper River Sidon, a proper "line" between Desolation and Bountiful, a proper land northward, etc.

If the geographic area involved spanned great distances, the task would be very difficult, if not impossible. Yet Book of Mormon geographers assure us that Book of Mormon events took place within a relatively small area, perhaps spanning only a couple hundred miles at most.

This conclusion was reached in the 1960s, hence the geographic setting of the Book of Mormon is recognized to have been a "local geography."[1]

Consider that many accounts simply refer to cities and lands in terms of "up" and "down" in elevation, in relation to each other. Directional terms like "over" (east or west) and "round about" are helpful. In some cases, distance factors are measured in terms of days of travel in a wilderness. Taken collectively, such terms and phrases can only offer clues.

When all is said and done, the exact locations of the cities and lands of the Book of Mormon may not seem to be important. Yet knowing that the Book of Mormon deals with real places and locations, can yield reassurance that its accounts took place in the real world.

Space will not allow discussion here regarding all the cites and lands presented on Map A, for the task is complicated to say the least. But, Appendix C presents references taken from the Book of Mormon that can provide some clues for ambitious readers who wish to accept such a challenge.

Please consider now some of the more interesting cities and geographical features.

The Waters of Mormon

The "waters of Mormon" were near a forest (Mosiah 18:30). And "there was in Mormon a *fountain of pure water* (Mosiah 18:5)."

Mormon was also "in the borders of the land having been infested, by times or at seasons by wild beasts (Mosiah 18:4)."

About fifteen miles north from Lake Chautauqua, at Cassadaga, are three tiny bodies of water, fed by water which comes up out of the ground like a spring, and other tiny inlet streams (see Map B). These small "lakes" at Cassadaga can be seen on a 1795 map of western New York, indicating that they were not man-made.[2] Marshlands border portions of each of these three small interconnected waters. It is easy to think of these waters as being a fountain.

These small bodies of water are fed by clear spring waters, that collect in the marshy area at the head of the top "lake." From there the water empties sequentially into one lake after the other by means of tiny interconnected channels. The stream then continues southeast to where it joins waters from Lake Chautauqua.[3]

It is interesting that these three small bodies of water could be referred to as "waters," in a plural sense, as in the "waters of Mormon."

The three small lakes at Cassadaga are set in a forested region of the uplands over-looking Lake Erie. This eastern shore region of Lake Erie was known in pre-colonial days for it's wild and ferocious beasts. Wolves, panthers (wild cats), bears, and other predatory animals once inhabited these wooded areas, making it hazardous to travel through the forests.[4]

This once coastal wilderness area seems to be a logical choice for the "west wilderness." The "wild beasts" which once infested this area seem to match the requirements found in Mosiah 18:4.

The Land of Helaman

Alma fled from the armies of King Noah in the land of Nephi and traveled eight days in the wilderness. "And they came to a land, yea, even a very beautiful and pleasant land, a *land of pure water* (Mosiah 23:4)." The name of the land was Helam.

On Map A the land of Helam is placed on a large creek, located in the vicinity of present-day Catteragus Creek, about thirty-five miles northeast of Lake Chautauqua. It seems likely that the city of Nephi may have been located somewhere in the vicinity of present-day Lake Chautauqua.

Such a distance seems consistent for a group of people, who may have been wandering in the wilderness for eight days, perhaps looking for a suitable place to dwell.

Consulting Map 9.1 one can also note that there were Indian villages on the eastern shores of the "west sea," with a concentration of sites found within the area of Catteragus Creek. Thus this seems like a good candidate for the land of Helam.

Cities in the Southwest Cluster

The development and establishment of cities in the land of Nephi apparently occurred first, since the land of Nephi was near to the "place of their fathers' first inheritance, and *thus bordering along by the seashore.*" (Alma 22:28). It appears most likely that this seashore was in reference to the "sea west" (Lake Erie).

Springfed, this small body of water at Cassadaga
(near Lake Chautauqua) feeds two others.
They are a good candidate for the waters of Mormon, "a fountain of pure water."

The Cattaraugus Creek area lies (south of Buffalo)
in the borders of "the west sea" (Lake Erie).
This may have been the land of Helam, "a land of pure water."

Presque Isle Bay is formed by a very small hook-like peninsula that juts out into Lake Erie, near Erie, Pennsylvania. Nowhere on the eastern seashore of Lake Erie is there anything like it. If the city of Jerusalem had been located on this tiny peninsula, it could have afforded defense by its strategic location, flanked by water on three sides. When the city of Jerusalem sunk in water at the time of the crucifixion (3 Nephi 9:7), perhaps Presque Isle Bay would have been formed where the city of Jerusalem once stood.

This site may be a reasonable site for the land of Jerusalem because of its association with proposed nearby lands of Mormon (Alma 21:1). The proposed land of Lehi-Nephi is assumed to be nearby, perhaps in Ohio, since this land was likely a land of first inheritance.[5]

Within the land of Nephi were a cluster of cities mentioned in Alma 23:9–12, which included the lands of *Ishmael, Middoni, Median, Shilom, Shemlon,* and the cities of *Nephi* and *Shimnilon.* Various accounts found in the Book of Mormon merely suggest the relative orientation of these lands and cities, with the terms "up," "down," and "over" helping to determine city locations found in the land of Nephi. The directional flow of rivers found in the area were also used in suggesting proposed city locations for the land of Nephi.

A Line of Possessions in the Southwest

Moroni received an epistle from Helaman telling him of the affairs in that "quarter of the land" (Alma 56:1). Helaman and two thousand young Lamanite men marched to the "support of the people in the borders of the land on the *south by the west sea [south]*" (Alma 53:8, 22). These young men were descendants of Laman, "who was the eldest son of our father Lehi," and they did march to the *city of Judea,* to fortify the city (Alma 56:9).

When Helaman arrived at Judea, he found that the Lamanites had "obtained possession" of the *land of Manti, or the city of Manti, and the city of Zeezrom, and the city of Cumeni, and the city of Antiparah*" (Alma 56:14). These cities may also have been a line of defensive possessions. Book of Mormon accounts are not clear about the location of these cities.

The city of Judea is proposed to be somewhat further north on the "line of possessions" because accounts indicate that it was a focal point in the south where Nephite reinforcements and supplies came "up" (southward) from Zarahemla. It was also the first city that Helaman arrived at in his campaign against the Lamanites (Alma 56:9, 15). The most likely route to the south may have been through the valley of Gideon to Judea, instead of through the rugged, high, "banks" of River Sidon, proposed to be just south of the land of Zarahemla.

When Helaman with his "little sons" marched near the city of Antiparah, "*as if we were going to the city beyond, in the borders by the seashore*," this was a decoy to lure the Lamanites out of the city of Antiparah (Alma 56:31). This suggests that Antiparah was on the river path leading directly to the chief city of Nephi, that may have been located near present-day Chautauqua Lake.

The account relating the Nephite capture of the city of Antiparah involved the use of a "stratagem." Helaman and his young men fled "northward" into the wilderness (Alma 56:36, 40, 42). The Lamanites were pursued in their rear by Antipus. When Helaman turned against the pursuing Lamanites, with Antipus in their rear, the Lamanites were captured in the wilderness. Prisoners were sent to the land of Zarahemla.

Another stratagem was employed to retake the city of Manti. Its proposed close proximity to the city of Judea is suggested from accounts found in the book of Alma. Readers might notice the role that the wilderness areas, suggested in Map 9.1, played in the recapture of the city of Manti (Alma 58:16–28).

Following battles to drive the Lamanites out of these cities, prisoners were taken "*down*" or north to Zarahemla (Alma 56:14–16). Note their proximity to Zarahemla on Map A.

Cities in the East

The Nephites began the foundation of a city called *Moroni*. This city "was *by the east sea; and it was on the south by the line of possessions* of the Lamanites" (Alma 50:13). Here the "east sea" is interpreted to be Cayuga Lake.

Examination of Map B should make it clear that Cayuga Lake is the largest of the Finger Lakes, on the east of the map. Oneida Lake

Presque Isle Bay, nearly surrounded by land,
juts out into Lake Erie, near Erie Pennsylvania.
Perhaps the city of Jerusalem, sunk at the crucifixion, was located here.

Sunrise on Lake Chautauqua. The city of Nephi may have been located
on the shore of this body of water in the southwest quarter of the land.

is not likely the "east sea" where the city of Moroni was built because it does not lie "on the south by the line of Lamanite possessions" (Alma 50:13).

Locating the City Moroni

If the proposed site for the city of Moroni is on the southern tip of present-day Cayuga Lake, considered as an "east sea," it would also be "in the borders by the seashore" (Alma 51:22).

Now the *city of Nephihah* was *"between the city of Moroni and the city of Aaron, joining the borders of Aaron and Moroni"* (Alma 50:14). It is likely that these three cities were near each other, in the south. The next verse states that they then began to "build many cities on the *north.*" The city of Lehi was by the "*borders* of the seashore."

A likely location for the city of Lehi was north of Moroni, along the northwest borders of the "east sea" (Cayuga Lake). Whether the city Lehi was to the east or to the west of such a proposed east sea, seems to be of little consequence.

Next, consider the placement of the city of Morianton in Map A. It is also in the east borders by the seashore. It is placed on the north of the "east sea" (Cayuga Lake), north of the land of Lehi (Alma 50:25). This is a strategic position because it suggests how convenient it would be for the people of Morianton to depart for the land northward (Alma 50:29).

The people of Morianton were met by the army of Moroni who did "head them off" at the borders of the land of Desolation (Alma 50:34).[6]

It is stated that the cities of Moroni, Lehi, Morianton, Omner, Gid, and Mulek were all possibly sequentially located "on the east borders by the seashore" (Alma 51:26). The location of these east borders can be seen from the following considerations.

The Lamanite Drive Northward

The Lamanites started a war offensive against Nephite cities, commencing with the city of Moroni in the south, and terminating with the city of Mulek in the north. Marching north the Lamanites took

Cuba Lake was formed from a small body of water.
As the "water of Sebus" (land of Ishmael), it would lie on a Zarahemla-Nephi path.

The Kinzua Dam lies within the Allegheny National Forest.
This land "down" south (Map A) is a good candidate for the land of Middoni.

possession of these cities with the destination of eventually reaching the land northward, most likely the land Desolation directly north of Zarahemla (Alma 51:28; Alma 52:2).

Lamanite armies were simultaneously marching "forth against the Nephites on the borders of the west sea." The Nephites were afraid that the Lamanites would have the "power to harass them on every side" (Alma 52:9, 12). Notice from Map 9.1 that it is also possible that "other cities" of the Nephites may have existed in the east, but they were not involved in the Lamanite offensive drive northward.

When the Lamanites began their siege of Nephite cities, they apparently by-passed the city of Nephihah, probably because it was so far south, and perhaps west, that its later capture was assured. Instead, the Lamanites were kept *"down"* by the seashore (Alma 51:25). The city of Moroni was their first real target city.

The Lamanites then proceeded to take possession of the cities of Moroni, Lehi, Morianton, Omner, Gid, and Mulek.[7] Notice on Map A that the cities of Lehi, Morianton, Omner, Gid and Mulek are so positioned in the borders by the seashore of a sea that the Lamanite armies advancing north, and then west, could capture these cities in sequence. However, the army of Teancum thwarted the Lamanite attempt to reach lands northward and the Lamanites had to retreat back to the city of Mulek (Alma 52:20).

The City of Mulek Challenge

The dilemma of the city of Mulek can be seen as follows. This city was *"one of the strongest holds of the Lamanites in the land of Nephi"* (Alma 53:6). Now, how could Mulek be in the land of Nephi, and yet be included in a Lamanite military offensive involving cities apparently in the east of Zarahemla? If Moroni, Lehi, Morianton, Omner, Gid, and Mulek were all placed in the borders of an "east sea," this would leave the Lamanite armies in the city of Mulek, to the east of Zarahemla. But could Mulek be east of Zarahemla and still be in the land of Nephi?

Map A suggests a solution for the challenge of the city of Mulek. By merely stringing out locations for the cities of Omner, Gid and Mulek as cities in the north, near the borders of the sea (eastern extension of Ontario Lake), running east to west, Mulek can be placed in lands associated with the land of Nephi. Thus the city of Mulek is located near a seashore as required, and also in the *north* to the land of Nephi.

To appreciate the significance of locating the land of Mulek where it is placed in Map A, we read that "the land *south* was called Lehi and the land *north* was called Mulek...for the Lord did bring Mulek into the land *north*, and Lehi into the land *south*" (Helaman 6:10). Here the directions "north" and "south" refer to the land of Nephi.

Thus the Lord may have led the Mulekites to lands in the north, not far from the southern shores of present-day Ontario Lake, whereas father Lehi may have been led to lands in the south of the land of Nephi, in the borders of the sea west, perhaps in what is today Ohio.

In the Nephite campaign to decoy the Lamanites from the city of Mulek, Teancum and his army marched *"down near the seashore"* (toward the sea on the north) while Moroni marched in the "wilderness, on the west of the city of Mulek." Reference is made to the *"plains"* which existed between the city Mulek and the city Bountiful.[8] When the Lamanites saw Teancum "retreat *down by the seashore, northward,*" they came out to pursue him, allowing the army of Moroni to take possession of the city of Mulek (Alma 52:20–22).

The Lamanites continued to pursue Teancum until they "came near the city *Bountiful* (this would have meant traveling east from Mulek). The proximity of the city of Bountiful to the city Mulek must have been sufficiently far that the distances "wearied" the Lamanites, "because of their march" (Alma 52:28, 31). Caught between Moroni's armies on their rear, and Teancum's on their front, the Lamanites were forced to surrender and were marched "into the land of Bountiful" (Alma 52:3), which was on the south of the borders of the seashore.

The City of Nephihah Challenge

The account of Helaman, with his two thousand young men, involves a "line of possessions," cities located in the southwestern quarter of the land. In their wars with the Lamanites, spies were sent out from the city of Judea to monitor the movements of the Lamanites so that the Lamanites did not pass them by and attack "other cities which were on the northward," probably referring to cities in the land of Zarahemla.

The Lamanite army "durst" not pass them and "march *down* against the city of Zarahemla; neither durst they *cross the head of Sidon, over to the city of Nephihah*" (Alma 56:25). This reference importantly establishes that the city of Nephihah was likely east from the head of the River Sidon. Here the term "over" suggests east of River Sidon.

The people of Nephihah had been gathered together "from the city of *Moroni and the city of Lehi and the city of Morianton*," suggesting that the city of Nephihah was not far from these cities. Lamanites displaced by the armies of Helaman, "from the land of Manti, and from the land round about, had come *over* and joined the Lamanites" and they began to attack the city of Nephihah. Moroni "saw that the city of Nephihah was lost" (Alma 60:5, 6, 11).

It was decided to drive the Lamanites out of the city Nephihah. Moroni and Pahoran, "leaving a large body of men in the land of Zarahemla, took their march with a large body of men toward the land of Nephihah, being determined to overthrow the Lamanites in that city." On the way to Nephihah, these men captured a "large body of men of the Lamanites," and "sent them to dwell with the *people of Ammon*" (Alma 62:17), in the land of Jershon.

At this time, the people of Ammon were living in the land of Jershon (see Map A). Notice that Moroni's journey to Nephihah from Zarahemla suggests that the Lamanite men were captured *south* of the land of Antionum, and sent north to dwell with the people of Ammon in the land of Jershon.

When Moroni and his men had come to the city of Nephihah, "they pitched their tents *in the plains of Nephihah, which is near the city of Nephihah.*" If the city of Nephihah was located near the southern portions of Seneca Lake, there are plains in the lands round about. From these plains, one can go "down" to the seashores of either Seneca or Cayuga lakes.

Entering the city by night, Moroni was able to obtain possession of the city of Nephihah (Alma 62:19, 26, 30). Moroni then "went forth from the land of Nephihah to the *land of Lehi*, which according to Map A, was not far from Nephihah.

A view of Cayuga Lake from the shore at Ithaca.
The city of Moroni, "by the east sea...on the south," may have been located here.

A view north from the southern shore of Seneca Lake at Watkins Glen.
The city of Nephihah, near a seashore, may have been located in this area.

Lamanites fleeing from Nephihah went "*down*" to the "borders by the seashore, until they came to the land of Moroni." "Down" makes sense because there is a highland area between Seneca and Cayuga lakes, in their southern borders.

Moroni, Lehi, and Teancum camped with their armies near Moroni so that the "Lamanites were *encircled* about in the borders of the wilderness on the *south*, and in the borders by the wilderness on the *east*" (Alma 62:31–34). Notice from Map A how the wilderness areas *around* the city of Moroni are suggested by these accounts. The Lamanites were driven out of the land.

The Hill Onidah

The name "*hill Onidah*" (O-ni-dah) is most interesting for it very likely can be associated with the name of one of the Iroquois Indian nations, the Oneida (O-ni-da). The names are pronounced the same. This is a uniquely New York name found in the Book of Mormon (Alma 32:4, 47:5).[9] The name may have been carried down through the centuries by Lamanites, to later generations of Indian peoples.[10]

The "hill Onidah" was where the prophet Alma went to teach the people. The great sermon Alma delivered on this hill has a parallel with the famous Biblical Sermon on the Mount. The "hill Onidah" is placed "*east*" of Zarahemla because when Alma and Amulek finished speaking, they came "over" (*west*) into the land of Jershon (Alma 35:1).

Amalickiah and a party left the land of Nephi and "went forward to the *place* which was called *Onidah*, for thither had all the Lamanites *fled…to Onidah*, to the *place of arms*." The story setting is given in Alma, Chapter 47.

The Oneida Indian name, according to historians, originated from the name, "*Oneota*," the name of the large stone found on the "*highest eminence*," (hill Onidah?), in the territory of their ancestral lands. Thus the Oneida were known as "the people of the stone."[11]

While the Oneida Indians historically occupied lands in central New York state, their ultimate origins are dated back into archaic times through recent studies in archaeology.[12] If their ancestors had occupied their ancestral lands far back in time, the name would have been known to the Nephites.

The shore of Cayuga Lake near Levanna.
A good candidate for the city of Lehi,
it was "in the north by the borders of the seashore."

A view of Oneida Lake at Brewerton, near Syracuse.
This area is a good candidate in which to place a "hill Onidah."

Thus the features of geography unique to the proposed New York setting for the Book of Mormon makes it possible to find answers to some puzzling locations for Nephite cities and lands. The internal consistency found by placing these cities and lands as shown in Map A seems to provide answers to some puzzling dilemmas of Book of Mormon city locations.

Readers are asked to take the time to carefully study the above considerations.

Endnote
(see Bibliography for references)

1. F.A.R.M.S (Sper-1983). This conclusion was reached by Sydney Sperry in 1963 in teaching Book of Mormon classes at BYU. While he was not the first to see that the Book of Mormon had a "local geography," his ideas on the subject eventually led to the theory that there must have been another Hill Cumorah located somewhere in the Central Americas.
2. The State of New York, "Compiled from the best Authorities," 1795, Cornell University Library Map Room, call number G 5800.
3. In the Bible, the "waters of Merom" were a lake formed by the river Jordan, a portion of which was a dense area of papyrus reeds. These waters are described as being "clear and sweet" (see Smith's Bible Dictionary, 1986). They give us an understanding of how "waters" might be interpreted as being a source, or fountain.
4. Ketchum (1864, 76-77).
5. It is a possibility that Lehi's party had first come to the shores of what is today Lake Erie in Ohio, perhaps near the site of Kirtland, Ohio. Remember that the Saints in the 1830s built the first temple of the restored Church in this location. It would seem to be fitting that the Kirtland Temple was built in lands that were anciently, Lehi's land of first inheritance.
6. Note that this event occurred at about 67 B.C., a time when many Nephites went to lands northward to the narrow neck of land. This may have been where the people of Morianton were headed because the land northward above the narrow neck of land is described as "covered with large bodies of water" (Alma 50:29).

7. This sequence of cities that the Lamanites proceeded to take possession of is suggested from their positions proposed in Map A. While this sequence is the author's own interpretation, it has also been previously proposed (see F.A.R.M.S., 1989, 32).

8. There are areas found within this region of western New York where "plains" once existed as large tracts of grassy land, which were undulating small hills. These plains are known to have once existed in western New York, probably far back into prehistory.

9. Other names found in the Book of Mormon that are found in New York today are Angola and Alma. In Pennsylvania is found the name Lehigh (pronounced Lehi). "Angola" in the 1830 edition of the Book of Mormon was Angela. The village of Alma and Alma Hill lies near the Pennsylvania border, about 15 miles south of Wellsville. The village of Angelica lies about 15 miles north of Wellsville. There appears to be no correlation between these names and the Book of Mormon. It is possible that the early Saints of western New York may have used Book of Mormon names in settlements in New York, just as the later Saints did when they arrived in Utah.

10. There is nothing out of place in finding an important Indian name of western New York that is used in the Book of Mormon. If Book of Mormon peoples had anciently occupied those same lands, it would be what one might expect. It is entirely logical that Lamanite descendants had carried the name Onidah down through the centuries, particularly when it was associated with a significant feature of geography, namely a place, a Hill Onidah.

    In translating the Book of Mormon it seems clear that the Prophet Joseph Smith would have recognized the name Onidah. After all, the well-known Oneida Indians lived about 100 miles east of Palmyra, N.Y. If the Prophet recognized this, he would have understood that Lamanite descendants, in his time, occupied lands not far from Hill Cumorah.

    This further suggests that the Prophet accepted Hill Cumorah as the site of the last battles of the Nephites, and would be consistent with his statements in the Zelph account that identifies Hill Cumorah as the site of those last battles.

11. Schoolcraft (1884, 93).

12. Fagan (1991, 415).

Chapter 11

Building Fortified Cities

SOON AFTER COLUMBUS ARRIVED IN AMERICA, SPANISH explorers set their sails northward from Florida, exploring the eastern coasts of the United States. In 1524 Jean de Verazzani reached what is today New York harbor. Their purpose was to find gold, but instead they found only that the land "contained hardly a road or a path that could be traversed without the cunning of a fox."[1] The United States and Canada presented a vast woodland wilderness, stretching from the Atlantic to the Pacific ocean, and occupied by a people who lived in the wilderness and who became known as the Indians.

The Plains

Teancum held a council of war with the Lamanite leader, Jacob, on the *"plains"* between the cities of Mulek and Bountiful (Alma 52:20). Understanding the nature of these plains, how they came about, and the role that they played in animal life can be seen as follows.

Found on the eastern seashore of Lake Erie today is the city of

Buffalo, located at the mouth of the Niagara River. William Ketchum in his 1864 *History of Buffalo* states:

> The earliest records and observations of those who visited the coasts of New England, before any permanent settlement of Europeans was made, represent the country for the most part as an *open prairie—made by the periodical burning over, of immense tracts of country by the native inhabitants.* The reason for this by Thos. Morton, in 1636, was, that it was for the *purpose of keeping down the growth of trees, shrubs, vines, and vegetation*, which would otherwise grow so rank as to become impenetrable and obstruct the vision, as well as the passage through it.[2]
>
> The inhabitants subsisted almost entirely by the chase; agriculture as a means of subsistence was entirely unknown to them. They lived almost entirely upon fish and the flesh of the animals they were able to kill by the means they then employed. They found it necessary to adopt some method to entice the graminivorous animals into the vicinity of their settlements, and by *burning the dried vegetation every spring*, they not only kept down the growth of timber and shrubs, but stimulated the *growth of a tender nutritious grass*, eagerly sought for by *the deer, the elk, the moose, and the buffalo*. These not only sought the luxuriant pastures for food, but they soon learned that these *open plains* afforded protection against their enemies of the carnivorous race of animals which prey upon them.[3]

Ketchum explains that all the regions of western New York contained "oak openings" which were once open prairies, and that these prairies extended over a large portion of the states of New York, New Jersey, Pennsylvania, Ohio, Kentucky, Tennessee, etc. Ketchum notes that the "plains" underwent a change in recent centuries.

Some readers of the Book of Mormon may wonder how it was that large numbers of Lamanites could find sustenance since they were known to live within the wilderness. A rich supply of easily obtained animals and fish was quite likely the key to their survival. The food-rich plains were possibly a great source of game, capable of supporting the numerous Lamanite populations. How animals mentioned in the Book of Mormon seem to fit into a western New York setting is explained as follows.

Animals in Nephite Accounts

Upon their arrival in the promised land, the Nephites found "in the wilderness, that there were beasts in the forests of every kind, both the cow and the ox, and the ass and the horse, and the goat and the wild goat, and all manner of wild animals, which were for the use of man" (1 Nephi 18:25).

Enos 21 states that the people of Nephi raised "flocks of herds, and flocks of all manner of *cattle of every kind, and goats, and wild goats*, and also many horses." About 17 A.D. reference is made in 3 Nephi 3:22 to "horses, and their chariots, and their *cattle*, and all their flocks, and their herds." Other references to animals are also found in 3 Nephi 4:4, and again in 3 Nephi 6:1.

Explorer Robert De La Salle passed through the regions of western New York in his 1680 journey from Quebec to the Illinois River. He reported: "The mountains are covered with *bears, stags, wild goats, turkey cocks and wolves*, who are so fierce as hardly to be frightened at our guns. The wild *bulls* are grown somewhat scarce."[4]

Notice the mention of goats and wild bulls. In 1 Nephi 18:25 it is mentioned that "goats" and "wild goats" were found in the land of promise and used by the Nephites (1 Nephi 19:25; Enos 21).

It is interesting to note that wild goats observed by La Salle in 1680 may have been still around some fifty years later. In 1723 John Steadman established a colony of goats on the tiny island located on the precipice of Niagara Falls, and it became known as "Goat Island." It may not be significant whether those goats were of a wild species, or not.[5]

In 1687 Louis De La Hontan journeyed along the south shore of Lake Erie and described: "I cannot express what *vast quantities of deer* and *turkeys* are to be found in these woods and in the vast meadows that lie upon the *south* side of the lake. At the bottom [south] of the lake we find *wild beeves [beavers?]…stags, roebucks and turkeys, run in great bodies* up and down the shore all round the lake."

Ketchum relates that from all accounts available, "we have descriptions of the *great numbers of wolves, bears, panthers, wild cats,* etc. which the early settlers encountered." He records that La Salle and his party, journeying through the region *south of Lake Erie* in the winter of 1680, encountered "*wolves* in such numbers as to be in danger of being overpowered by them." It was not safe to "even pass through this country."

Ketchum's references agree with accounts found in the Book of Mormon that describe the land of Mormon, located in the borders of Nephi (Alma 5:3), and "being in the borders of the land having been infested, by times or at seasons, by *wild beasts*" (Mosiah 18:4). The proposed land of Mormon (see Map A) well fits this wild beast description.

Cattle Explained

In 1637 Thomas Morton, one of the early settlers of New England, published an account of the Indians using buffalos that inhabited the vicinity of Lake Ontario.

> They [the Indians] have also made description of *great herds* of well-grown beasts, that live about the part of this Lake Erocoise, [now Lake Ontario] such as the Christian world, until this discovery, hath not been made acquainted with. These beasts are of the bigness of a cowe, *their flesh being good food*, their hides good leather, their fleeces very useful, being a kind of woolle, and the savages do make garments thereof.[7]

Ketchum relates that Father La Moine, who visited the Onondagas in 1634, says: "Traveling through vast prairies we saw in divers quarters immense *herds of wild bulls and cows*, their horns resemble in some respects the antlers of a stag....Droves of twenty cows *plunge into the water as if to meet us*."[8] Please note the phrase, *cows in the water*: it will be demonstrated that these words, spoken in French, lies at the root of the name "buffalo."

In 1718 M. De Vaudrael, in a memoir of the Indians of Canada, wrote that "Buffaloes abound on the *south* shores of Lake Erie, but not on the north." In 1721 Charleviox spoke of the *River aux Boeuf*, which became known as Buffalo Creek, a few miles east of the entrance to the Niagara river, on Lake Ontario.

"Boeuf" is a French word for *beef*.[9] Also, the French word "aleau" (pronounced ah-low) literally means "in the water."[10] Thus "boeuf," coupled with "aleau," sounds as "buff-alo," which by the early French explorers would have meant "beef in the water."

It is generally believed that domesticated cattle did not exist in the
pre-Columbian Americas. But the American Bison that roamed the
prairies of North America are considered cattle. It is noteworthy that
since these cattle (buffalo) were found in rich abundance within the
proposed Book of Mormon lands of Map A, the Nephites very likely
made use of them, as well as raising cattle of other kinds (Enos 21).

Mention of Horses

While it is mentioned that horses and chariots were possessed by
King Lamoni (Alma 18:9, 20:6) and by Governor Lachoneus (3
Nephi 3:22), it appears from many accounts that the movements of
Nephite and Lamanite armies occurred on foot. Perhaps dense wood-
lands with limited trails made use of the horse quite limited except in
certain locations where highways and roads existed.[11] Perhaps only
Kings and Governors and certain leaders made use of them.

In 1687 the Baron De La Hantan was surprised to find "plenty of
horses, black cattle, fowl and hogs" in the villages of the Seneca Indians
of western New York.[12] Since colonial laws strictly prohibited trade
between the Indians and the Colonists, it is doubtful that the horses
were obtained from the colonists. It was also observed that in 1725 the
Cherokee Indians were found to be using horses, of a species different
from that used by the Spanish.[13] While these matters still require further research, they support the Book of Mormon's claim that the
Nephites did possess horses.

Seeds of Every Kind

Before the colony of Lehi departed into the wilderness, they took
with them "seeds of every kind" (1 Nephi 16:11). Upon arriving in the
promised land, they began to till the earth and to plant the seeds that
they had "brought from the land of Jerusalem" (1 Nephi 18:24).

The record of Zeniff states that the ground was tilled with "all manner of seeds, with seeds of *corn*, and of *wheat*, and of *barley*, and with
neas and *sheum*, and with seeds of all manner of fruits" (Mosiah 9:9).

It is known that the Indians of Illinois made use of small starchy
seeds, called "little barley" (Phalaris caroliniana). Perhaps these small

seeds were the barley referred to in the Book of Mormon.[14]

Corn, wheat and barley are recognized as crops that grow well in temperate climates. The area of western New York has a temperate climate and there is no problem with accounts that state that the Nephites grew these crops.

Mention of "neas" is interesting. Quite likely the intended word was *"peas."* An examination of the handwriting of Oliver Cowdery reveals that his writing of "p" looks a lot like an "n," perhaps causing the printer to print the word "neas." The other possibility is that since "neas" sounds a lot like peas, Oliver may have recorded it that way.

If the word really intended was peas, then this is another temperate climate crop that the Nephites grew.

It is not known what "sheum" was. However, the Hebrews prepared "shew-bread," which was an unleavened bread eaten on the Sabbath (Exodus 25:30). When newly baked, it was ritually sprinkled with incense and placed in the sanctuary for one week. Perhaps "sheum" was in reference to spices or leaves, "sheum," grown for the incense. Notice that the reference in Mosiah 9:9 does not refer to "sheum" as a seed.

Nephite Houses of Cement

In a land northward of the narrow neck of land, Nephites dwelt "in tents, and in houses of cement." They lacked "timber to build their houses," their cities, temples, synagogues, sanctuaries and other buildings. In this land northward, they built "many cities of both of wood and of cement" (Helaman 3:9, 10).

Some have wondered about this mention of the use of cement. North American Indians were known to bend tree saplings over, forming a structure that could be covered with other sticks, all tied together forming a tightly woven shell. Various muds or clays were then applied, allowed to dry, until a rather rigid structure resulted. Could such structures be considered to have been made of "cement"?

Possibly the Nephite definition of cement was more like mud or clay mixed with grass or straw, dried until it became hard. Such a cement, applied to structure of wood, might have formed a house of cement.

Nephite Wooden Cities

Several passages suggest that the Nephites built cities of wood. Many Nephite cities were burned when Christ was crucified. The Lamanites also burned Nephite cities.

In *An Approach to the Book of Mormon*, Hugh Nibley states:

> The most significant fact about both Jaredite and Nephite cities is not that they were great or fortified or rich or proud, but that they were *built*. A city would be planned and built all at one time, like a house. Cities were not the product of a slow gradual accretion from hamlet to village to town to city to metropolis...but if we believe the Book of Mormon, they were *built up all at once*.[15] (italics added).

An important consequence of building wooden cities is their deterioration over time. If Nephite towers, temples, synagogues, houses and buildings were made exclusively of wood, and not of stone, in the times after the Nephites were gone, the Lamanites may have replaced rotting wood with new timber.[16] Thus some Nephite cities may have been maintained by the Lamanites, while others gradually rotted away.

Nephite Fortified Cities

Moroni began "erecting small forts, or places of resort...throwing up banks of earth round about...also walls of stone...all round about the land" (Alma 48:8). Nephites fought the Lamanites with stones and with arrows, their strongest men using swords and slings. Thus Moroni built "forts of security, for every city in all the land round about" (Alma 49:2, 13, 19, 20).

It is well known that prehistoric western New York was covered with sites of fortification, evidence that some previous inhabitants engaged in battles using these forts. It is generally believed that these forts were erected by the Iroquois Indians, who are supposed to have occupied the area only as far back as the 11th or 12 centuries A.D.

But some of the more recent anthropologists hold that the "Iroquoians go back to Archaic times...before 2500 B.C." Latter-day Saints might find this interesting to contemplate, as the Book of Mormon relates a continuous possession of the land, from the Jaredites to the Mulekites and Nephites, spanning back into this same time period.

A most interesting reference to Nephite fortifications is mentioned: "Upon the top of these ridges of earth, he (Moroni) caused that there should be timbers, yea, works of timbers built up to the *height of a man*, round about the cities" (Alma 50:2). Interestingly, these structures of timbers and works of earth are described almost exactly by early explorers, in their accounts of early New York Indians.

The picture on the next page was taken from the works of William Beauchamp, *A History of the New York Iroquois*. It is a sketch made by Champlain of The Onondaga Fort, which is found in the New York State museum.[18] The sketch shows a *tower* overlooking a works of *pickets*.

Nephite fortified cities contained a "breastwork of timbers." "And he [Moroni] caused that upon those works of timbers there should be a frame of *pickets* built upon the timbers round about; and they were strong and high. And he caused *towers* to be erected that overlooked those works of pickets" (Alma 50:4).

When La Salle first visited a Seneca village in 1669, he noted that: The village had "palisades 12 or 13 feet high, bound together at the top and supported at the base behind the palisades by large masses of wood and of the *height of a man*."

It is notable that La Salle's description corresponds so well with the description given in the Book of Mormon. The descriptions of ruins of ancient fortifications mentioned by McGavin and Bean, taken from many sources, are consistent with these Book of Mormon descriptions.[19]

Because Nephite fortifications described in the Book of Mormon correspond so well with those once occupied by Indians of the New York area, it can be inferred that these Indians quite likely were Lamanite descendants who retained the Nephite practice of fort-building, over many generations. In the period following the last battles at Hill Cumorah, the Lamanites continued to be "at war one with another" (Mormon 8:7).

It is important to recognize the implications of the ancient fortifications found in western New York by the early explorers and colonists. Instead of seeing these fortifications only as the work of the Iroquois Indians, their significance can go much deeper. It is perfectly reasonable that the Iroquois Indians merely followed the fort building practices originated by their forefathers, the Lamanites.

Nephites built a framework of pickets with towers (Alma 50:4)

Engraving from Champlain's "Voyages and Discoveries, 1615–1618."

Used with permission (Rare Books Division, The New York Public Library; Astor, Lenox, and Tilden Foundations).

In Mormon 8:8 it is mentioned that following the last battles at Hill Cumorah, the Lamanites were "at war one with another… and no one knoweth the end of the war." Thus it may have been that the Lamanites continued to battle each other using the concepts of fortification utilized by their ancestors.

Ancient fortifications were found all over western New York. What more appropriate place might there be where one could expect to find the ancient forts of the Nephites?

Endnote
(see Bibliography for references)

1. Schoolcraft (1885, 12).
2. Ketchum (1864, 16).
3. Ketchum (1864, 17).
4. Ketchum (1864, 76–77).
5. Dow, vol.1 (1921, 393). It is reassuring to find that in ancient times goats once occupied proposed Book of Mormon lands. Goats are rugged animals and it is generally acknowledged that they have helped supply human needs since prehistoric times.
6. Ketchum, op. cit.
7. Ketchum, (1864, 83–84).
8. Ketchum, op.cit.
9. Webster (1986, 158). See "boeuf bourguignon" (beef of Burgundy).
10. Eric Delton, of Sacramento and a recent immigrant from France, helped clear up this interpretation. Eric did not know of any French word ending in "alo," but he was aware that, in sound, "aleau" meant literally "in the water." From this I was thus able to suggest that the name Buffalo is derived from the French, "beef in the water."
11. The term "highway" might be misunderstood in terms of modern-day use. Concrete highways probably should not be imagined as we know them (3 Nephi 6:8). "Casting up" a highway may have simply meant building up roadbeds through the use of landfill and rocks over irregular terrain, or possibly through marshy or wetlands.
12. Howard (1965, 29).
13. Thompson (1992, 336).
14. Fagan (1991, 360).

15. Nibley (1957, 346).
16. There appears to be a lack of evidence that stone was significantly used for building cities in ancient North America. Evidence is that wooden temples were built on earthen platforms. Monuments constructed to honored dead were made of earth, and tombs were constructed of timbers. Some stone was used in constructing tombs in periods which could be identified as being post-Nephite.
17. Fagan (1991, 415).
18. Beauchamp (1968, Plate 11).
19. See McGavin and Bean (1948, 55, 60, 76, 77, 81, 85). On page 85, Francis Parkman (Jesuits in North America, p. 29) describes an Iroquois fort. His description involves a ditch, several feet deep, with earth thrown up on the inside. By burning trees and using stone hatchets, the builders created palisades, in one, two, three or four concentric rows, made to intersect each other.

"The whole was lined within, to the height of a man, with heavy sheets of bark; at the top where the palisades crossed, was a gallery of timber for the defenders, together with wooden gutters, by which streams of water could be poured down on fires kindled by the enemy. Magazines of stones, and rude ladders for mounting the rampart, completed the provisions for defense."

Chapter 12

Scattering of the Lamanite Seed

WHEN THE BOOK OF MORMON CAME FORTH IN 1830, the early Saints had no difficulty in identifying the Indians as Lamanite descendants. After all, the Indians they saw looked much like the Lamanites described in the Book of Mormon. The Lamanites in B.C. 178 are described as having "their *heads shaved*, that they were *naked*; and they were girded with a leathern *girdle* about their loins," a "blood-thirsty people" (Mosiah 10:8, 12).

In B.C. 87 the Amlicites "marked themselves with *red* in their *foreheads* after the manner of the Lamanites." The *"heads* of the Lamanites were *shorn*; and they were *naked*, save it were skin which was *girded* about their loins..." (Alma 3:4–5).

Apparently this style of Lamanite dress continued down over centuries, for in A.D. 18 the Lamanite Gadianton robbers still "had a lamb-skin about their loins, and they were dyed in blood, and their heads were shorn, and they had head-plates upon them" (3 Nephi 4:7).

Lamanites marked their foreheads red and had their heads shorn (Alma 3:4).
Picture by Charles Bird King.
Used with permission of the National Collection of Fine Arts.

Lamanites were naked, except for a skin which was girded about their loins (Alma 3:5).
Used with permission of Louis S. Glanzman, artist.

The nomadic Indians lived in *wigwams* (tents) and hunted in the forests. This Indian way of life was observed by the first European settlers. The Lamanites were described as "wild and ferocious... dwelling in *tents*, and wandering about in the wilderness...and their skill was in the bow, and in the cimeter, and the ax" (Enos 20).

In the centuries following first contact between the Indians and the Europeans, the Indians began to adopt features of European dress, even though they still retained much of their traditional style. Bone breastplates and headplates, bows and arrows were retained, while stone clubs were replaced with iron axes and muskets, beginning in the early 1600s. These were received in exchange for furs offered by the Indians to the frontier trappers and traders. It is said that an Indian would travel 1,000 miles to acquire a war hatchet made of iron.

The Wentworth Letter

The Prophet Joseph Smith wrote a letter to newsman John Wentworth. It was first published in the *Times and Seasons* in 1842. The letter has been described as "one of the choicest inspired documents ever written."[1] The Wentworth letter, in part, sets forth the events and circumstances surrounding the coming forth of the Book of Mormon and the early rise of the Church.[2] In this letter are found the following significant and interesting statements of the Prophet.

> I was also informed concerning the aboriginal inhabitants *of this country*, and shown who they were, and from whence they came, a brief sketch of their origin, progress, civilization, laws, governments, of their righteousness and iniquity, and the blessing of God being finally withdrawn from them as a people was made known unto me.[3]

Stating that America in ancient times had been inhabited by two distinct races of peoples, the Prophet then goes on to state:

> The principal nation of the second race fell in battle towards the close of the fourth century. The remnant are the Indians that now inhabit *this country*. This book also tells us that our Savior made his appearance upon this continent after his resurrection.[4]

At the time when the Prophet wrote these statements he was living in Nauvoo, Illinois. The statement "this country" obviously refers to the United States, a country consisting of lands eastward from the Missouri River. Illinois had been made a state a little over twenty years before Nauvoo was built.

Taken in their broadest context, these statements indicate that the Prophet saw the Indians of North America as Lamanite descendants, "remnants" of the seed of Jacob.

Mission to the Lamanites

In September 1830, four months after the Church was organized, Oliver Cowdery's mission to the Lamanites is reiterated: "I have given unto him power to build up my church *among the Lamanites*" (D&C 30:60). Parley P. Pratt was to accompany "my servants Oliver Cowdery and Peter Whitmer, Jun., into the wilderness among the Lamanites" (D&C 32:2).

Where was this wilderness? A clue is found where the Lord states that "this church have I established and called forth out of the wilderness" (D&C 33:5). At the time when the Church was established in 1830, New York was part of a western frontier that reached from the Appalachian Mountains westward to the western edge of the Missouri River.

In October 1830, Oliver Cowdery, Peter Whitmer, Parley Pratt, and Ziba Peterson departed on their mission to the Lamanites, then living south of the city of Buffalo, New York, in the area of the Catteragus Creek. Of these Indians, these missionaries recorded that they had been "instructing them in the knowledge of *their forefathers*."[5]

These early missionaries first went to the area of Catteragus Creek, about 30 miles south of the city of Buffalo. Map A suggests that this was the ancient land of Helam, a "land of pure water" (Mosiah 23:4).

After "they bade adieu to their brethren and friends," they "commenced their journey, preaching by the way," until they came to Kirtland, Ohio, where they remained for some time.[6] According to ideas proposed in a previous chapter, these missionaries may have passed into Lehi's land of first inheritance, coming to the area of Kirtland, Ohio, where the first temple of the restoration would be shortly built.

From Ohio, the first missionaries made their way to the western borders of the State of Missouri. In 1843, in addressing the Pottawattami Chief at Council Bluffs on the Missouri River, a wilderness to where the Indians had been forcibly driven, there the Prophet Joseph Smith made the following important statement: Referring to the Book of Mormon, he said, "*This is the book which your forefathers made. I wrote upon it.*"[7]

This statement leaves little room for doubt that the Prophet saw these people as Lamanite descendants.

Then in May 1844, while addressing the Sac and the Fox Indians in Nauvoo, the Prophet Joseph stated: "*The Great Spirit* has enabled me to find a book [showing the Book of Mormon] which told me about *your fathers.*"[8] Perhaps like their Lamanite ancestors, these Indians readily understood the meaning of the term Great Spirit, mentioned in Alma 18:2, 11, 18, 28.

Scattered by the Gentiles

Nephi made a prophecy concerning the promised land and the peoples who would inhabit this land. "The Lord God will raise up a *mighty nation among the Gentiles*, yea, even upon the face of this land; and by them shall our seed be scattered" (1 Nephi 22:7).

This prophecy found fulfillment by the scattering of the Indians of the eastern United States and Canada by the early colonists, through population pressure and by government edict. The Indians were forced to leave their homelands in the eastern U.S. and migrate to regions further West. In 1830–40, Indians of the Cherokee, Chickasaw, Choctaw, Creek and Seminole tribes were forcibly removed to what later became the state of Oklahoma. There they were joined by Indians of many other tribal affiliations.

Notice that reference is made to a "mighty nation" that was *raised up among the Gentiles*. There is no other nation in the Americas that could qualify for being the mighty nation like the United States. If not the United States, then what other mighty nation? To claim that this statement referred collectively to all the nations of the Americas does not seem likely in the context of 1 Nephi 22:7.

Please notice that this mighty nation would scatter the seed of Nephi. Such scattered "seed" could only refer to the Indians of North

America. Nowhere else in the Americas have Indian peoples been "scattered," to the extent suggested, and specifically by a mighty nation of the land, like the Indians of eastern United States and Canada.

Gentiles to Possess Land

Nephi also foresaw that the land of promise would attract people from other countries: "A land which is choice above all other lands...and the Lord hath covenanted this land unto me, and to my children forever, and *also* all those who should be *led out of other countries* by the hand of the Lord" (2 Nephi 1:5).

Here it can be seen that the promised land was not only for the children of Nephi, but also for those "led out of other countries." Also, "The Lord hath reserved their blessings, which they might have received in the land, for the Gentiles who shall possess the land." Furthermore, "They shall be driven and scattered by the Gentiles; and after they have been driven and scattered by the Gentiles, behold, then will the Lord remember the covenant which he made..." (Mormon 5:19–20).

There is nowhere else in the Americas, except in the United States and Canada, where Gentiles have so completely "possessed" the land of Lehi's children in fulfillment of this prophesy.

No Place for an Inheritance

In speaking to Lehi, the Lord said: "This land should be kept as yet from the knowledge of other nations; for behold, many nations would overrun the land, that there would be *no place for an inheritance*" (2 Nephi 1:8). The Lord warned Lehi that "if the day shall come that his children would *reject* the Holy One of Israel...he will bring other nations unto them...and he will *take away* from them the lands of their possessions, and he will cause them to be *scattered* and *smitten*" (2 Nephi 1:10, 11).

The prophecy was that if the seed of Lehi should reject Jesus Christ, then other nations would come to occupy the lands promised to the seed of Lehi. The Savior did come to visit the Nephites and Lamanites in these lands. But Lehi's children, Nephites and

Lamanites, eventually did reject Christ, the Holy One of Israel. Thus, the land of their inheritance eventually became overrun by those of other nations.

In colonial times the French, the English, the Dutch, and the Swedes came to occupy these lands. While the first settlers in both the United States and Canada were from these nations, eventually peoples from many other nations flooded the shores of these lands, to the point that the seed of Lehi indeed had no place for an inheritance, in fulfillment of prophecy.

Lamanite Remnant after Scattering

When the Nephites first came to America, they probably found their land of inheritance only periodically traveled by wandering tribes. Perhaps only aboriginal hunters occasionally passed through their lands for seasonal camping. These migratory peoples probably only occupied the extensive woodlands of the area, living off fish and animals, possessing many of the same cultural features later acquired by the descendants of Laman and Lemuel, shortly after their arrival in America (2 Nephi 5:24).

Archaeologists tell us that ancient America contained native peoples who would have also inhabited North America for thousands of years prior to the coming of the Nephites. Also, Book of Mormon accounts mention that the Lamanite populations grew much more rapidly in number than those of the Nephites, even from the very beginning.

This suggests that the descendants of Laman and Lemuel probably intermarried with natives of the land, quickly creating a kinship with the native population that lived in surrounding lands. Thus over the period of the Nephites, the Lamanite populations became much larger than those of the Nephites. Such an idea is not without parallel, for also the children of Israel came to dwell among various "ites," intermarried, and served their idol gods (Judges 3:5–6). Even though the number of Lamanites may have been very large, the number of Lamanite survivors following the death and destruction that occurred at Cumorah may have been smaller than one might think. The estimated loss of a quarter of a million of Nephites must have surely been accompanied by a correspondingly even greater loss among the

Lamanite armies. Typically the Nephites inflicted heavy losses among the Lamanites.

The destruction of the Nephites at Cumorah occurred because of their fallen spiritual state.[9] That the surviving Lamanites at Cumorah may have been relatively small in number is implied by Moroni. In referring to these Lamanites, he mentions that they were "a *remnant* of this people who were spared" (Mormon 7:1).

Thus the scattering of the Lamanite seed can be seen to have commenced immediately following the battles at Cumorah. Moroni notes that "the Lamanites are at war one with another; and the whole face of this land is one continual round of murder and bloodshed" (Mormon 8:8). These wars undoubtedly further reduced the ranks of the remaining Lamanites.

In consequence the remaining Lamanites likely suffered great losses in their internal wars following Cumorah. A greatly reduced Lamanite population thus made it easier for their seed to be scattered and absorbed into other native Indian populations in regions bordering the land of promise. These Indian populations of eastern North America may have quickly become diffused with the seed of the Lamanites. In this way Lamanite customs became lost among the native Indian populations, causing the Indians to retain only semblances of the customs and traditions of the Lamanites.

This explanation seems consistent with knowledge that so many different Indian tribes of North America had such different language dialects when first discovered by the European colonists.[10] The language of the Lamanites became like those of the much more numerous Indian tribes into which they became absorbed. Thus any remnant of the Lamanite language, either written or spoken, may have become very diffuse and only faintly distinguishable among some Indian tribes of North America by the time of the first Europeans.[11]

In this sense, the Indians tribes of North America that absorbed the Lamanite seed became the "remnant" of the seed of Jacob.

Death by Fire

Death by fire was a Lamanite practice. "They should suffer, even death by fire" (Mosiah 19:20). Lamanites who became converted were to "perish by fire because of their belief" (Alma 25:5). The prophet Abinadi "suffered death by fire" at the hands of King Noah (Mosiah 17:14–20).

The culture of the Iroquois Indians of western New York was a culture of many similarities with that of Book of Mormon peoples. These included building fortified cities with palisades, painting their foreheads in red, wearing a girdle about their loins, possessing name endings in "hah," dwelling in tents, and other characteristics not uncommon to many other Indian peoples. But the Iroquois possessed the peculiar practice of "burning" their enemies.

The Iroquois Indians executed their victims by having their captives run barefoot through a gauntlet of red hot coals, prodded on by a jeering crowd who poked at the victims with flaming sticks. Sometimes victims were ritualistically burned by attaching ropes of flaming pitch to their bodies that produced slow torture. Painful burning at the stake was also a common practice that was used.

Thomas Henry mentions that it was only the Iroquois Indians of New York, among all the eastern Woodland Indians who executed by fire.[12] Might these Indian peoples have inherited the practice from Lamanite forefathers, a remnant that had once inhabited their lands?

Feeding upon Flesh

Moroni reports that following the last battles at Cumorah, the Lamanite survivors had "lost their love, one towards another; and they thirst after blood and revenge continually" (Moroni 9:5).

Moroni states that the Lamanites took many prisoners, men, women, and children. After slaying the men, the Lamanites then fed "the women upon the flesh of their husbands, and the children upon the flesh of their fathers" (Moroni 9:8).

These gruesome acts were further added upon by the even more wicked Nephites. After taking daughters of Lamanite prisoners, they then proceeded to torture their bodies, and to "devour their flesh like unto wild beasts" *as a token of their bravery.* Moroni saw the depravity of his people, stating that "tongue cannot tell, neither can it be written" the horrors of their perversion (Moroni 9:9–24).

The Mohawk Indians who occupied the region of the Mohawk

River valley of central New York were so named because the name "Mohawk" means "man eaters."[13]

The tribes of the Iroquois Indians treated their captives with utter brutality of the most inhuman kind. After killing a man, they would "tear out his heart, roast it on coals, and distribute it in pieces to the young men; *that they think this renders them more courageous.*"[14] Other tortures and beastly acts are recorded in historical accounts.

These items reinforce the thesis that the Indians of the eastern woodlands had adopted wicked Nephite and Lamanite ways. However, while the cultural center of the Nephites is identified in the area of western New York (see Map A), both Nephite and Lamanite practices were far reaching in their effects on later generations of the Lamanites seed.

Lamanite Legends?

Aside from the visit of the Savior to the Nephites in ancient North America, there may be evidence that he also later visited other Israelites then living in the Central Americas. To support this, there are well-known legends of a visit by a Great White God to the peoples of that area. It is possible that these people were other of Christ's sheep, people who he told the Nephites he would later visit?

Speaking to the Nephites of these "other sheep," the Savior said: "I have other sheep which are not of this land [of the Nephites], neither of the land of Jerusalem, neither in any parts of the land round about whither I have been to minister...I go to show myself to them" (3 Nephi 16:1–3).

Is it reasonable that the Lamanites, after Cumorah, would have carried forth legends of Christ's visit to the Nephites? It seems doubtful for the following reasons.

At the time of the destruction of the Nephites at Hill Cumorah, the Lamanites were "without Christ and God in the world" (Mormon 5:16). "And because of their hatred, they put to death every Nephite that will not deny the Christ" (Moroni 1:2).

It seems hardly likely that Lamanite descendants, anti-Christs, would carry forth legends of the visit of a Christ whom they hated. Following the destruction of the Nephites at Cumorah the Lamanites wanted nothing to do with Christ.

For many Latter-day Saints, Indian legends of a Great White God, Quetzalcoatl, are appealing and suggestive that the resurrected Savior had visited the Central Americas.[15] While some aspects to the legends may be based in fact, much controversy surrounds the subject, and many books have been written about the legendary figure Quetzalcoatl.[16]

Thus legends of a Great White God that have any basis in a visit by the Savior to the peoples of the Central Americas in ancient times, could only have resulted from his visit to other Israelite peoples, other lost sheep of the House of Israel who were not Lamanite descendants. If Christ had visited these other Israelites, they could have retained legends of his visit to them.

According to the thesis of this book, Christ's visit to the Nephites would most likely have occurred in those same lands where he returned to appear to the Prophet Joseph Smith in 1820.

Endnotes
(see Bibliography for references)

1. McConkie (1966, 834).
2. Jessee (1989, 429). In this reference the letter is given in it's entirety. The letter was published in the 1 March 1842 issue of the *Times and Seasons*.
3. Jessee, loc. cit.
4. Jessee, loc.cit.
5. Joseph Smith vol.1, (1978, 120).
6. Joseph Smith, vol.1 (1978, 118–120).
7. Joseph Smith, vol. 5 (1978, 480).
8. Op. cit., vol. 6, 402.
9. Near the Grand River of western Missouri, not far from the site of Adam-ondi-Ahman, the Prophet Joseph Smith named a site as Tower Hill, "in consequence of the remains of an old Nephite altar or tower that stood there." (Joseph Smith vol.3, 1978, p.35). This incident suggests that Nephites may have traveled far and wide. It also seems to be consistent with the Zelph incident, wherein a Lamanite warrior and chieftain was buried on the banks of the Illinois River, having died

from wounds inflicted during "the last great struggle of the Lamanites and Nephites" at Hill Cumorah (Joseph Smith vol.2, 1978, p.80). Thus while the Book of Mormon describes events associated with a rather localized geographic setting, this does not rule out that over the centuries both Nephite and Lamanite peoples may have spread far from the lands proposed in Map A.

10. It is estimated that when the Europeans first arrived in America, 300 native languages were spoken in North America. According to modern studies on Indian language classifications, these languages can be grouped into linguistic families. In the United States and Canada seven linguistic families are identified, in the Central Americas the number is set at 70, while in South America the number is only three (Grolier, vol.10, 1991, 86).

The issue of the great number of Indian languages has challenged some Book of Mormon scholars (Roberts, 1985, 21). It was seen that the great diversity of Indian languages had occurred in too short of a time period after AD 400, in order for all the Indian tribes of North America to have been Lamanite descendants. While Roberts offers no real explanation for this dilemma, the ideas presented in this chapter are intended to offer a reasonable explanation.

11. It goes beyond the scope of this book to deal with the subject of Indian languages and writing. While there is no consensus that the Indians of North America ever had a written language, there are some evidences that some Indian tribes did have a written language long before the coming of the European colonists.

12. Henry (1955). Please note the "hah" ending in the name of the Mohawk Indian leader, Hiawatha, who is credited with founding the Five Nation Iroquois League. He should not be confused with the legendary Hiawatha of Henry Longfellow's poem. Names of other noted Iroquois Indians ended in "hah," as do Book of Mormon names such as Nephihah and Moronihah. James Adair (1968), in the 1760s, pointed out that his study of Indian nouns reflect their use of the Hebrew "hah," which he takes as an "accent of admiration."

13. Reaman (1967, 25).

14. Scheele (1950, 44).

15. Talmage (1952, 289). Talmage quotes President John Taylor: "We can come to no other conclusion than that Quetzalcoatl and Christ are the same being."

16. Sertima (1976, 73–76). Sertima presents evidences that images of Quetzalcoatl are distortions stemming from a visit of an African Mandingo king and his company, all wearing white robes of royalty. Temple wall inscriptions seem supportive of the theory. On the other hand, Gordon (1971), 51–52, has found Old World archaeological evidences that compare favorably with New World Indian traditions.

Chapter 13

The Last Battles at Cumorah

T HE CONDITION OF THE NEPHITES AT ABOUT 50 BC
was that the righteousness of the people had greatly deteriorated
in the land of Zarahemla. Gadianton robbers began to be established
in the land, under the leadership of Kishkumen. Lamanites had come
into the midst of the Nephites. Samuel, the Lamanite, prophesied
that a great destruction would come upon the Nephites at the time of
Christ's crucifixion, because of their great wickedness.

Destruction at Crucifixion

At the time of the crucifixion of Christ, great destruction came
upon the Nephites and Lamanites. There were storms, tempests,
thunder, and lightnings. Key events are recorded in the chapters of
third Nephi.

Some propose that volcanos had to be involved in the destruction.
But the destruction is described as a "great storm," and as a "terrible
tempest...terrible thunder...sharp lightnings..." followed by fire.
Cities sunk in water, and earth covered up others. This all happened
"because of the tempest and whirlwinds and thundering and the

lightnings, and the exceeding great quaking of the whole earth," suggesting earthquakes (see 3 Nephi 8:5–8).

It is also mentioned that people were "overpowered by the vapor of smoke and of darkness…these deaths and destructions by fire, and by smoke, and by tempests and by whirlwinds, and by the opening of the earth…" were in fulfillment of prophesy (3 Nephi 10:13–14).

People can and do die from smoke inhalation as a result of fires. Whirlwinds can cover things up with earth, and tornados kill people by the havoc which they wreak. One might imagine a volcano being involved, but these accounts do not require volcanos. If the destruction did occur in the New York area as proposed, it is not likely that volcanos were involved since there are no volcanos in this area.

But what about earthquakes and tornados? Are they possible for this part of the land? Tornados are not unheard of in eastern North America. They can sometimes occur, but are not on the scale of strength that the prairies of western United States sometimes spawn.

In the area of Lake Ontario and Lake Erie can be found a region of identifiable possible earthquake activity. It is possible that a quake of magnitude 6 or 7 on the Richter Scale could occur within this region, with a projected frequency of about once in 1500–2000 years.[1] Thus, there is a possibility for a sizeable quake at the death of the Savior for the narrow neck of land region at Niagara.

It is assumed that in spite of the great destruction that occurred to cities and lands, the basic features of geography were not altered to where the basic geography of the Book of Mormon became indistinguishable. Most Book of Mormon scholars agree that such an assumption is reasonable.

Nephite Cities and Lands in the North

Locations for cities and lands north of Zarahemala, prior to the destruction of the Nephites at Hill Cumorah, are derived from accounts taken from Mormon, chapters 1–8.

When Mormon was ten years old, Ammaron hid up the records that contained the history of the Nephites. Mormon was instructed that "when ye are about twenty and four years old…go to the land *Antum*, unto a *hill* which shall be called *Shim*…and take the plates of

Nephi unto yourself, and the remainder shall ye leave in the place" (Mormon 1:3).

Hill Shim was possibly in the near vicinity of Hill Ramah/ Cumorah, as implied from mention of it in Ether 9:3, where Omer "came over and passed by the hill of Shim, and came over by the place where the Nephites were destroyed." It seems likely that Hill Shim would have been just *north* of the land of Zarahemla, based upon the idea that Hill Cumorah was not far from Zarahemla (see Chapter 5).

Please note the following sequence of events and refer to Map 13.1, presented on the following page, for the discussions that follow.

1. At age eleven, Mormon reports that he was "carried by my father into the *land southward*, even to the land of Zarahemla." From Map 13.1 it is seen that Zarahemla is proposed to be south of the land of Cumorah. Perhaps Mormon and his family had been residents of the land of Cumorah prior to Mormon being carried southward.

War began between the Nephites, including Jacobites, Josephites and Zoramites, and the Lamanites that included Lemuelites and Ishmaelites. It began in the borders of Zarahemla, by the waters of Sidon. More than 30,000 men of the Nephites succeeded in defeating the Lamanites. Gadianton robbers among the Lamanites began to infest the land (Mormon 1:1–18).

2. Mormon, age 16, became head of the Nephite army. The Nephites would not fight and they began to retreat to the north countries above Zarahemla. These countries were quite likely north of Zarahemla, perhaps in the land of Bountiful on the north, as well as within the land Desolation that lay north of Bountiful, in the borders of the sea on the north. And it came to pass that they "did come to the city of *Angola*."[2] Perhaps this city was a short distance north and west of Zarahemla (Mormon 2:4).

3. Then, after being driven out by the Lamanites, Mormon's army moved to where it was driven "forth out of the land of *David*" (Mormon 2:5), likely continuing toward the north countries.

4. His armies still being pursued by the Lamanites, Mormon relates that; "And we marched forth and came to the land of *Joshua*, which was in the borders *west* by the seashore" (Mormon 2:6). It is suggested here that this seashore was that of a "sea west," south of the narrow neck of land (Lake Erie).

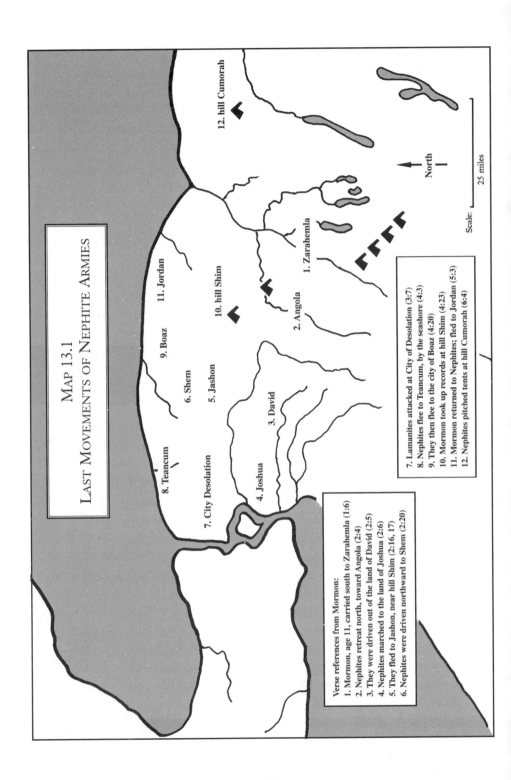

MAP 13.1
LAST MOVEMENTS OF NEPHITE ARMIES

12. hill Cumorah

North

Scale: 25 miles

11. Jordan

10. hill Shim

9. Boaz

6. Shem

5. Jashon

1. Zarahemla

2. Angola

3. David

8. Teancum

7. City Desolation

4. Joshua

7. Lamanites attacked at City of Desolation (3:7)
8. Nephites flee to Teancum, by the seashore (4:3)
9. They then flee to the city of Boaz (4:20)
10. Mormon took up records at hill Shim (4:23)
11. Mormon returned to Nephites; fled to Jordan (5:3)
12. Nephites pitched tents at hill Cumorah (6:4)

Verse references from Mormon:
1. Mormon, age 11, carried south to Zarahemla (1:6)
2. Nephites retreat north, toward Angola (2:4)
3. They were driven out of the land of David (2:5)
4. Nephites marched to the land of Joshua (2:6)
5. They fled to Jashon, near hill Shim (2:16, 17)
6. Nephites were driven northward to Shem (2:20)

150

At this time the strength of the Nephite army was about 42,000 war-riors, while the Lamanite strength was 44,000 (Mormon 2:9).

5. After many wars with the Lamanites, the Nephites were pursued until they came even to the land of Jashon. The city of Jashon was near the land Antum where Ammaron had deposited the records. Note that Hill Shim was located near the land of Antum.

6. The people of Nephi were again hunted and driven. They were driven forth until they came *northward* to the land which was called *Shem*.

At this time the strength of the Nephite army was 30,000 warriors, while the Lamanite strength was 50,000 (Mormon 2:25).

Notice that the size of the Nephite army declined while that of the Lamanites increased.

7. What happened next is significant. After many trying battles with the Lamanites, the Nephites had their lands of inheritance divided. "And the Lamanites did give unto us the land *northward*, yea, even to the *narrow passage* which *led* into the land *southward*. And we did give unto the Lamanites all the land southward." (Mormon 2:28, 29).

This account suggests that from this time onward, the Nephite armies were confined to cities and lands located northward above the Escarpment ridge, within the land of Desolation, northward above the "line" that separated the lands of Bountiful and Desolation.

The "narrow passage" mentioned was most likely the natural path provided by the ridge of the Niagara Escarpment. While the Escarpment runs west to east (or vice versa), it represented a well-traveled path leading from Zarahemla to lands northward, including those found above the narrow neck of land.

8. Mormon gathered his people together at the land *Desolation*, to a city which was in the borders, by the narrow pass that led into the land *southward*. The Lamanites came *down* to the city of Desolation to battle (Mormon 3:5–7), but the Nephites beat them.

This reference to coming "down" to the city of Desolation is interesting for it suggests that the city of Desolation was likely located down, or north, below the Escarpment. Possibly the Lamanites occupied highlands on the Escarpment ridge, which could have been as much as 200 feet above the seashore at the Niagara River area. This idea is reinforced by the account mentioned in Mormon 4:1 where the

Nephites went *"up"* to "battle against the Lamanites, out of the land Desolation."

9. The city of *Teancum* lay in the borders by the seashore and it was also near the city Desolation. In battles the Nephites fought the Lamanites, and did "drive them out of their lands" (Mormon 4:15). A series of see-saw battles between the cities of Desolation and Teancum occurred. The results were great losses for the Nephite armies. The Nephites were "swept off...as a dew before the sun" (Mormon 4:18).

10. When the Lamanites came against the Nephites in the city of Desolation, the Nephites fled until they "came to the city *Boaz*" (Mormon 4:20). The city Boaz may have been to the east of the city of Desolation.

11. When Mormon saw that his people were being overthrown, he went to the *Hill Shim*, where he took up *all* the records that Ammaron had hid up. This may have meant that Mormon was not far from Hill Shim on the east, which in turn was not far from the land Cumorah. Mormon no longer wanted to lead his people.

After removing *all* the records from Hill Shim that Ammaron had hidden up (Mormon 4:23), Mormon returned and was again given command of Nephite armies (Mormon 5:1). The amount of records that Mormon removed from Hill Shim must not have been too extensive because it seems that he carried them with him in his battles.

The implication is that when Mormon finally placed these records in Hill Cumorah, they most likely were joined together with a volumous amount of other records, all of which would remain there until the days of the Prophet Joseph Smith.

12. When the Lamanites again came against the armies of Mormon, the Nephites fled to the city of *Jordan*. Other cities were also maintained by the Nephites as strongholds, cutting off the Lamanites such that "they could not get into the country which lay before us" (Mormon 5:4). The site for the city of Jordan may have been on some large creek or stream, not far from the Escarpment ridge, since a name association suggests a river, as in the "Jordan River." A possible site near the Escarpment ridge suggests a defensive location.

In a series of battles between Nephite and Lamanite armies, Nephite towns and villages were burned by the Lamanites. So great were the numbers of the Lamanites, that they did tread the Nephites under their feet. Those who could not escape before the pursuing Lamanites were swept down and destroyed (Mormon 5:7). Thus the armies of the Nephites were defeated and confusion occurred as they fled from the Lamanites.

13. Mormon wrote an epistle to the king of the Lamanites desiring that the Nephites "might gather together our people, unto the land of *Cumorah*, by a hill which was called Cumorah." Remember that Cumorah was "in a land of *many waters, rivers, and fountains*" (Mormon 6:4). There the Nephites hoped to gain an "advantage" over the Lamanites.

What possible advantage might Mormon expect to win over the Lamanites by gathering his people in the land of Cumorah? First, note that this land Cumorah was apparently well known, otherwise how would the Lamanites recognize it? Perhaps the advantage that Cumorah offered was its value as a spiritual center, more than anything military.

Hill Cumorah was likely located near a site of Nephite population in the land Bountiful. It may have been part of an important city-center, such as the city Bountiful (see Map A). A Nephite temple may have once stood on Hill Cumorah's promontory, or nearby. A repository for ancient records is believed to have been located inside the hill.[3]

Not all the Nephites went into lands northward. Accounts relate it was Mormon's armies that were driven into the "north countries." The elderly, women and children, families of the warriors most likely remained behind. Thus, if Cumorah was below the narrow neck of land, and not above, not far north of Zarahemla, then the land of Cumorah would offer a definite advantage as a place for remaining Nephites to gather. Those who gathered at Cumorah would have included Nephite people from the land of Nephi in the south, those by the sea in the east, those still remaining in the land of Zarahemla, and those remaining in lands northward above the narrow neck of land.

Mormon records that "we had gathered in all the remainder of our people unto the land of Cumorah" (Mormon 6:5). This suggests that the many battles with the Lamanites in the "north countries" had involved the Nephite armies that Mormon commanded.

Since the Nephites had lost great numbers of their 42,000 warriors in battles in the north countries, and since Mormon commanded 10,000 men at Hill Cumorah (Mormon 6:10), it is reasonable that only 10,000 warriors survived the battles with the Lamanites in the north countries.

It appears that Mormon only had 10,000 battle-seasoned Nephite warriors remaining after his wars with the Lamanites in the north countries.

Toward Cumorah

The Nephite armies marched forth to the land of Cumorah, under a reprieve from the Lamanite king, and pitched their tents *around about* the Hill Cumorah. Note the term "march" implies armies of warriors. Had there been women and children involved, it seems unlikely that they would have "marched" to Cumorah (Mormon 6:1).

The land of Cumorah is described as "a land of *many waters, rivers, and fountains*" (Mormon 6:4). Most likely "waters" refer to large bodies of water such as seas or lakes, creeks or rivers, and water falls or fountains. The lands of Hill Cumorah in New York matches such a description.

Hill Cumorah lies within the Finger Lake region, wherein lie eleven large lakes, plus many other smaller bodies of water. All these Finger Lakes drain northward into Lake Ontario by means of interconnected rivers or creeks. There should be little doubt that the land of Cumorah in New York satisfies Book of Mormon descriptions.

Also, note the term "around about" suggests a rather singular hill, a hill with a promontory. From the promontory of Hill Cumorah in New York it is possible to have a nearly 360 degree view of surrounding lands.[4]

Eventually other men, women and children were all gathered together into the land of Cumorah. It took about four years to gather in *all* the remainder of the Nephites, while still under the reprieve of the Lamanite king (Mormon 6:5).

Mormon hid up in Hill Cumorah the plates of Nephi and all the records with which he had been entrusted (Mormon 6:6). Thus the scene was set for a great last battle at Hill Cumorah.

Nephites did pitch their tents "around about" Hill Cumorah.
From the top of Hill Cumorah Mormon witnessed the destruction of his people.

Looking west from Hill Cumorah, as seen in the early 1950s.
From here one could easily imagine great battles involving many thousands of people.

The Destruction of the Nephites

Seeing the approaching armies of the Lamanites, Mormon record-ed: "And it came to pass that *my people*, with their *wives and their children*, did now behold the armies of the Lamanites marching toward them" (Mormon 6:7). "Every soul was filled with terror because of the greatness of their numbers" (Mormon 6:7–8). The implication is clear that a slaughter would involve *all* of the Nephites, both men, women and children.

"And it came to pass that they did fall upon *my people* with the bow, and with the arrow, and with the ax, and all manner of weapons of war." Mormon then goes on to explain how his people were destroyed in increments of ten thousand, each under the leadership of one man (Mormon 6:11–14).

Mormon referred to the 10,000 warriors under his command as "my men...my ten thousand who were with me" (Mormon 6:10). These men were remnants of an army of 42,000, nearly wiped out in previous battles with the Lamanites.

Mormon states that "when they had gone through and hewn down *all my people*" there were only twenty-four left. On the morrow when the Lamanites had returned to their camps, Mormon and the twenty-four survivors beheld the slaughter that had occurred. The implication is that each unit of 10,000 involved *people*, rather than 10,000 male warriors in each unit.

The last battle at Cumorah had been a death struggle for all the Nephites, every man, woman and child, in units of 10,000. This is supported in verse 19 where Mormon cries; "O ye fair sons and daughters, ye fathers and mothers, ye husbands and wives, ye fair ones, how is it that ye could have fallen." From this it is clear that those Nephites slain at Cumorah consisted of a total of 230,000 men, women, and children, all the Nephite people.

From the top of Hill Cumorah, Mormon and his companions could have easily witnessed the destruction of the 230,000 Nephite men, women and children, that occurred in the surrounding lands.

Thus the Nephite civilization came to and end and all the Nephites were destroyed. The few who escaped into the south countries were hunted down and destroyed, and a few dissented over to the

Lamanites.

Reflecting upon the 230,000 Nephites who were slain at Cumorah one can see that this was not really very many Nephites who had been spread over the lands of the Book of Mormon. However, the large numbers of Lamanites, after their great losses at Cumorah, were probably still quite large.

Lamanite survivors of Cumorah were left to possess Nephite cities and lands, living in a depraved state of perpetual wars.

Endnote
(see Bibliography for references)

1. Nishenko and Bollinger (1990, 1413-1416).
2. Hauck (1988, 105). Hauck calls attention to the name Angola, stating that in the original 1830 edition of the Book of Mormon, p. 520, Angola was spelled "Angelah."

   It is interesting that Angola State Park lies today just south of the city of Buffalo, New York, along the seashore of Lake Erie. Its name can be traced to 1839, when Angola was established as a post office village associated with Evans Station. The village of Angelica lies today near the Genesee River, in Allegheny County. Angelica had been a county seat, having been established in 1805. (see Morrison's Annals of Western New York (Ovid: W.E. Morrison & Co., 1975).
3. Readers may recall that the Prophet Joseph Smith and Oliver Cowdery had visited a room inside Hill Cumorah, wherein they saw wagon-loads of ancient records (details of the account were presented in Chapter 2). Readers might also contemplate that the Manti, Logan, and Bountiful, temples in Utah were also built on a commanding position, high on a hill above the valley below.
4. It has been suggested that the Hill Cumorah in New York is too small to match Book of Mormon requirements. One factor related to this would be the size of the armies involved. Estimates that millions of people were involved in the last battles appear not justified according to the analysis presented in this chapter. If Hill Cumorah and the plains surrounding it were anciently devoid of tree, which most likely they were, then there would be no problem with Mormon witnessing the total destruction of the Nephites from the top of Hill Cumorah.

Chapter 14

Return to Cumorah

THE EVENTS ASSOCIATED WITH THE COMING FORTH OF
the Book of Mormon are well known in Church history.
However, when re-examined in the light of the New York geography
presented in this book, they take on new meaning and significance.
Let us now briefly consider some of these events to see if they appear
to be merely coincidental happenings, or if they reveal a pattern of
divine purpose.

Joseph to "Rise Up"

About 590 years before Christ, the Prophet Lehi stated to his son
Joseph that, "I am a descendant of Joseph who was carried captive
into Egypt (2 Nephi 3:4)." This Joseph of Egypt, who was the twelfth
son of Jacob (Israel), had two sons, Ephriam and Manasseh. These
two sons of Joseph were blessed by Joseph's father Jacob, and thus
were considered as tribes of Israel.[1] Lehi was a descendant of
Manasseh (Alma 10:3).

In 2 Nephi 3:15, Lehi relates that Joseph of Egypt saw the day when the Lord would raise up yet another descendant through Joseph's son, Ephriam, and that his name would be called after Joseph of Egypt. This descendant, Joseph Smith Jr., rose up as *"one mighty among them,"* among Lehi's descendants, "bringing to pass much restoration unto the house of Israel" (2 Nephi 3:24).

In 1816 the Smith family moved to Palmyra, New York, which is identified in Map A as being in the land of Bountiful. Joseph was about eleven years old at that time, the same age that Mormon was when he was carried into Zarahemla by his father. It seems to be no mere coincidence that young Joseph Smith would grow up in the midst of Lamanite descendants, of whom the Book of Mormon accounts speak.

Thus Joseph Smith, in fulfillment of prophecy, did "rise up" in the midst of the descendants of Lehi in the land of Bountiful, and brought them knowledge of their fathers.

The Savior in Bountiful

According to accounts found in the Book of Mormon, Jesus Christ appeared in the New World to the righteous Nephites and Lamanites, following his resurrection in Jerusalem in the Old World. His visit occurred at the temple found in the land of Bountiful (3 Nephi 11:1–10). There he established his Church, with twelve apostles, among the Nephites. Following his visit to the Nephites in Bountiful, Christ "departed" (3 Nephi 28:12).

Since Jesus Christ "departed" from among the Nephites in Bountiful, perhaps one might expect that Christ would again return to the land of Bountiful, where the restoration of gospel blessings could be brought to Lehi's seed. Joseph Smith's account of the "First Vision" states that the Father and the Son, Jesus Christ, appeared to him in 1820, in the Sacred Grove. The Sacred Grove probably lies in what was anciently the land of Bountiful.

Translating the Book

Most of the manuscript for the Book of Mormon was translated in Harmony, Pennsylvania. It was there that Joseph and Oliver were baptized and received the Aaronic Priesthood. These are great historic events that were part of the restoration of the Gospel. There may be something noteworthy in that Joseph moved to Harmony, where these events occurred.

The Book of Mormon was translated, Joseph and Oliver baptized, and the Aaronic Priesthood restored, all in these lands which were located in a "south wilderness" which may have been anciently occupied by Lamanites, to whom the Book of Mormon was written.

Printing the Book

Martin Harris mortgaged his farm so that 5,000 copies of the Book of Mormon could be published in 1830. The printing of the Book of Mormon occurred in the village of Palmyra, not far from the home of Joseph Smith.

What more appropriate place might there be where the Book of Mormon should have come forth than in Palmyra, almost within the shadow of the Hill Cumorah? The Book of Mormon was published in what may have been the land of Bountiful, where significant events recorded in the Book of Mormon are assumed to have taken place.

Early Baptisms

On April 6, 1830, the Church of Jesus Christ of Latter-day Saints was organized in the village of Fayette, Seneca County, New York, at the home of Peter Whitmer. The new church consisted of six members. Fayette lies only a couple of miles from the northwest seashore of Cayuga lake.

There seems to be significance in these events occurring near the place where the ancient Book of Mormon city Lehi may have been located in 71 B.C., lying in the north by the "borders of the seashore" of an "east sea" (Alma 50:13–15). Thus it may be that the Church of Jesus Christ of Latter-day Saints was organized in lands bordering upon the ancient land of Zarahemla.

Seneca Lake lies about twenty-five miles southeast of Palmyra. Here in June 1829, some of the first convert baptisms occurred. Joseph baptized his brother Hyrum Smith, and David Whitmer, while Oliver Cowdery baptized Peter Whitmer, Jr. in this lake.[2]

Mission to Lamanites

The title page of the Book of Mormon states that it was "Written to the Lamanites." Early Church members believed that the Lamanites were the ancestors to the Indians then found in eastern North America. Four months after the first conference of the Church in June 1830, four missionaries were dispatched on the first mission of the Church, a mission to the Lamanites.

These missionaries headed west and first visited the Cattaraugus Indians living near Buffalo, New York.[3] In Map A the Cattaraugus Creek area, along the shore of Lake Erie, is identified as being part of the land of Helam.

It would seem quite appropriate that the message of the Book of Mormon was first taken to Lamanite descendants then living within the lands of the Book of Mormon. The first missionaries to the Lamanites in 1830 brought the message of the Book of Mormon to Indians then living in what may have been anciently part of the land of Nephi.

The First Temple

Kirtland, Ohio, lies in the borders of Lake Erie, about one hundred miles southwest of Lake Chautauqua. This places Kirtland within the "borders" of the ancient land of Nephi, possibly within the land of Lehi's first inheritance (see Map A). Kirtland was "the city of the Stake of Zion" (D&C 94:1).

It may be no mere coincidence that the first temple of Christ's restored church may have been built within the borders of what was anciently the land of Nephi. The first temple of the restoration was dedicated in 1836, on the shores of a "west sea," in the land of "Shinehah" (D&C 82:12). These lands in Ohio may have been where father Lehi first arrived, in his land of promise, and even perhaps where he died and was buried.

Hill Cumorah Pageant

Each year since 1937, one of America's foremost pageants, "America's Witness for Christ," is held on the hillside of Hill

The LDS ward chapel on the Cattaraugus Indian reservation,
south of the city of Buffalo.
First mission to the Lamanites was here in 1830.

Joseph Smith, 1843:
"The Great Spirit has enabled me to find a book which told me about your fathers."
Permission of BYU Museum of Art.

Cumorah, near Palmyra, New York. This pageant has drawn crowds numbering in tens of thousands annually.[4] The pageant depicts scenes from the Book of Mormon.

In the memorable pageant scene where the destruction at the time of the resurrection is portrayed, it is stirring to contemplate that this destruction had occurred on location, in Nephite days. It is also moving to see portrayed in the pageant the visit of the Jesus Christ to the Nephites. Striking is the realization that this most likely occurred in this land of Cumorah where the pageant is presented.

There seems to be no other place in America that could be a more fitting location to hold a pageant which depicts the ancient peoples of the Book of Mormon, than on location, at the actual site where events found in the Book of Mormon occurred. How appropriate it is that the pageant, "America's Witness for Christ," portrays the visit of Jesus Christ to the Nephites, in lands where he likely visited them. Most inspiring is a visit to the promontory of the Hill Cumorah, where it is possible for one to share the view that Mormon had, as he witnessed the entire destruction of his people, the Nephites.

A Modern Temple

In 1990 a temple was dedicated at Toronto, Canada, across a sea on the west, across from the Hill Cumorah. In October General Conference of that year, Thomas Monson of the First Presidency, gave his closing remarks concerning the 1990 dedication of the temple in Toronto, Ontario, Canada. He concluded with the remark that one could look from Toronto, Canada, across Lake Ontario all the way to Hill Cumorah. President Monson noted that high on top of the temple in Toronto is a statue of Moroni, as found on many Mormon Temples. Regarding this statue he remarked: "I noted that in Moroni's hand was his familiar trumpet. He was gazing homeward—homeward to Cumorah."[5]

It seems quite fitting that a temple has been established in Canadian lands, across a "narrow neck of land," in a "land northward." If the lands of the Book of Mormon are even closely approximated as given in Map A, the above considerations provide some things to ponder.

Another View of Cumorah

In light of all the above, there must be something much more significant about Hill Cumorah than has heretofore been realized. Hill Cumorah is likely more than simply a hill where the Prophet Moroni buried the ancient records from which the Book of Mormon was written.

We can get a better glimpse of the importance of the land of Cumorah by recognizing that it lies within what was once a Bountiful wilderness. According to 3 Nephi, chapter 11, the resurrected Savior appeared to the multitudes gathered together at the temple that was built within the land of Bountiful. It is reasonable that the temple where Christ appeared to the Nephites may have also been at or near the important city of Bountiful.

When we contemplate these ideas, perhaps we can better understand just why Mormon chose to gather in all the remaining Nephites for a last great battle at Hill Cumorah. This might have been because Hill Cumorah was located in a key portion of the land of Bountiful. It is possible that the great ancient city of Bountiful had stood within the land of Cumorah. As a wilderness area, Bountiful was an extensive area, within which other cities and lands existed.

It is conceivable that the temple of the Nephites, to which the Savior came, may have been near, or even associated with Hill Cumorah itself. Somehow this seems to fit with the idea that the First Vision in 1820, where the Father and the Son appeared to the boy Joseph Smith, occurred a mere two miles from Hill Cumorah, within that Bountiful wilderness.

We can only imagine that Nephite cities had once existed near Hill Cumorah. And we can only imagine the significance of a Nephite temple located in Bountiful. Regardless, one thing still remains: we can hereafter find a much more special place in our hearts for that Hill whose significance we can perhaps only catch a glimpse of.

A Return to Cumorah

If one were to visit an Onondaga Indian "longhouse" found in central New York today, there one could expect to find fourteen Onondaga Chiefs who sit in council, each sharing opinions in matters concerning their nation, as their forefathers of old did.[8]

Today the chiefs of a small Confederation of Six Iroquois Nations are presided over by a kind of speaker of the house, a Chief among the Chiefs. When these chiefs meet, their speaker holds in his hands a ceremonial staff of office, an eagle-headed cane of authority.

The founder of the centuries-old confederacy was called the Peacemaker.[9] The words of the founder are believed to be:

> Think not forever of yourselves, O Chiefs, nor of your own genera-
> tion. Think of continuing generations of our families, think of our
> grandchildren and of those yet unborn, whose faces are coming from
> beneath the ground.[10]

Let us consider that in years to come some Latter-day "Chief among the chiefs" might relate to his people about a great ancestor who had preserved ancient records of their forefathers, whose voice had spoken from the ground. This voice from the ground tells of their forefathers who had fought in a last great battle with Nephites at Hill Cumorah.

The story about this great man, in some time in the future, may possibly be told as follows.

> Morning rays of the rising sun cut their way through the early mist
> which lay hovering over the quiet waters of a great sea. A man, weary of
> 35 years hiding out and avoiding capture, made his way along the
> seashore, carrying a cloth-wrapped bundle under his arm. This is
> Moroni. He had been over this terrain in the past. Now, he was making
> his way to a very special place...Hill Cumorah.
>
> In his travels that day, he had seen smoke from a campfire trickling
> upward, signaling to him that there were Lamanites in the area and that
> he must still be watchful. It reminded him of the many times that he had
> seen columns of smoke rising from the cities that the Lamanites had
> burned. When he reached the Hill Cumorah that evening it was sunset.
>
> On top of Hill Cumorah, as his eyes swept the panoramic view before
> him, a flood of memories came to his recollection, like haunting sounds
> out of the distant past. The shouts of men and women as they battled in
> defeat, and the mournful cries of children swelled his heart with sorrow.
> His feelings of sorrow surfaced again as he recalled the destruction of his
> family and people.

He recalled the voice of his father, who had commanded him to write a few things about his people. Painful was his recollection that his father had been killed by the Lamanites, and that he had been left alone to tell the sad tale of the destruction of his people.

In the morning he had a chore to perform. He must bury the records in their final resting place in Hill Cumorah. As the last rays of the sun sunk beneath the horizon he knew that sleep was not long in coming. He did not know how long he had yet to live. But the Spirit whispered to him, that in some future day…he would again return to Cumorah.

Moroni returned to Cumorah on September 23, 1823.

Endnotes
(see Bibliography for references)

1. McConkie (1966, 808).
2. Ibid, 103.
3. Joseph Smith, vol.1 (1978, 118–119).
4. On some Pageant nights, it was not unusual to find an audience of 30,000 people near the foot of Hill Cumorah, including those in parked cars. This occurs only on one side of Hill Cumorah, in a rather small area, compared to the much larger area surrounding this hill. One should have no difficulty at all in imagining 230,00 Nephites and probably many more than that number of Lamanites being destroyed in the general area around Hill Cumorah.
5. Monson (1990, 70).
6. Lying today within relatively obscure farmlands in the state of Illinois, stands a hill of rather singular appearance. It was once covered with trees and hardly discernable, but today it is bare. What is more, the hill is not a hill at all, but it is an ancient burial mound. This important archaeological site near St. Louis, Missouri, was not explored until recent times. Today it is known as Cahokia, the largest burial mound complex found in North America. Lying about 75 miles north of Cahokia, on the banks of the Illinois River, is the known site which the Prophet associated with Zelph.

   Sometime around A.D. 700, about 300 years after the demise of the Nephites at Hill Cumorah, this gigantic mound was built through the efforts of thousands of workers, carrying dirt in baskets.

   On top of the principal mound in Cahokia, stood a religious edifice, referred to as a temple. This principle mound was once the spiritual focal point for over 10,000 inhabitants who occupied the site at its peak occupation. Cahokia endured until about A.D. 1200.

What is known today is hardly more than speculation as to whom the ancestors of these peoples were, why they came there to live, and why they became extinct.

Haunting is the realization that perhaps Nephite cultural influences could have been carried down through generations of Lamanite descendants, reaching many points in the United States, far beyond the cradle of Nephite lands, once located in the New York area.

7. McGavin and Bean reported, quoting much of Turner's findings, that "in 1922, on the Rose Farm, one half mile from Mormon Hill a number of large skeletons, stone implements, copper ornaments, a copper axe of unusual type, and other articles were found. At this historic spot were found many [skeletons] of unusual physique, tall, long-limbed, finely shaped."

"In 1925 a farmer near Palmyra was digging a cellar and found several large skeletons...." The Rochester Museum "estimated the ages of these giant skeletons to be at least 3,000 years old."

"Turner describes a fortified hill within three miles of the Hill Cumorah which was barricaded on an eminence, made for a large and powerful enemy. It must have been a very valuable place for defensive warfare. The entrenchment ten feet deep and twelve feet wide was plainly visible to the first settlers in that region."

"The skeletons that were found within the enclosure of this fortress and in the immediate vicinity indicate a race of men one-third larger than the present race. A few miles away hundreds of skeletons of both sexes and all ages were found within an enclosure. This had been the theatre of sanguinary battle, terminating in favor of the assailants."

While it might be difficult to equate these findings directly with Book of Mormon peoples, they seem to support of the idea that important events had anciently taken place in the land of Bountiful proposed in Map A.

8. Some of this information was related to this author by Oli Gibson, one of the 14 chiefs of the Onondaga Nation, in a personal interview in June, 1993.

9. Historians believe that this peacemaker was a Mohawk Indian leader named Hiawatha. "Iroquois tradition romanticizes the historical Hiawatha as a semimythical culture hero" (Grolier Encyclopedia, 1991).

10. Arden (1987, 370-403).

Appendix A

Other Proposed Maps

Over the decades since the Book of Mormon was first published, students of the Book of Mormon have attempted to determine where the Nephites had lived. Earliest thinking was that Book of Mormon peoples had lived over most of North, Central and South America. The narrow neck of land at Panama was believed to be the one mentioned in the Book of Mormon. However, about the turn of the century it became recognized that Book of Mormon events must have taken place in a much more confined area. But it was not until the 1930s that the first maps began to appear, suggesting a rather limited geographic setting for the Book of Mormon.

In 1990 FARMS published a Study Aid written by John Sorenson, *The Geography of Book of Mormon Events: A Resource Book* (FARMS document SOR-90c). Presented in Sorenson's work is an analysis of some sixty-eight works of various scholars over the years that have suggested geographic models for the Book of Mormon. Of these works, Sorenson identified nine that can be considered as "internal," those supposedly derived independently of any real-world interpretations. Interested readers are invited to examine Sorenson's *Resource Book* for more details.

Internal Maps

An analysis of the various "internal" maps reveals some general features of geography. These features have been studied, summarized, and are presented here as a composite, Map A1, found on the next page. While some differences are noted in different maps, Map A1 is intended to represent the general features of geography derived by those who attempt to create an internal map. While the differences typically exit in the placing of certain cities and lands, this is to be expected because in some cases the Book of Mormon gives us little to go on.

Most geographers recognize that the Book of Mormon mentions cities in the east, by the seashore, and cities in the west. Other cities can be associated with the River Sidon, etc. Some geographers refer to these cities as city complexes, or see them as clusters because the Book of Mormon suggests their close proximity to each other.

These internal maps can only be expected to be approximately correct. However they can serve as guidelines in general features of geography that should be consistent with any real world setting that is proposed.

Five internal maps have been chosen that can be considered as representative. They cover most of the general features in geography that can be derived from Book of Mormon accounts. The specific features of the five maps are summarized and presented in Table A1, following Map A1. Readers might also refer to Map A, front cover of this book, and compare how well these "internal" maps match the New York geography presented in this book.

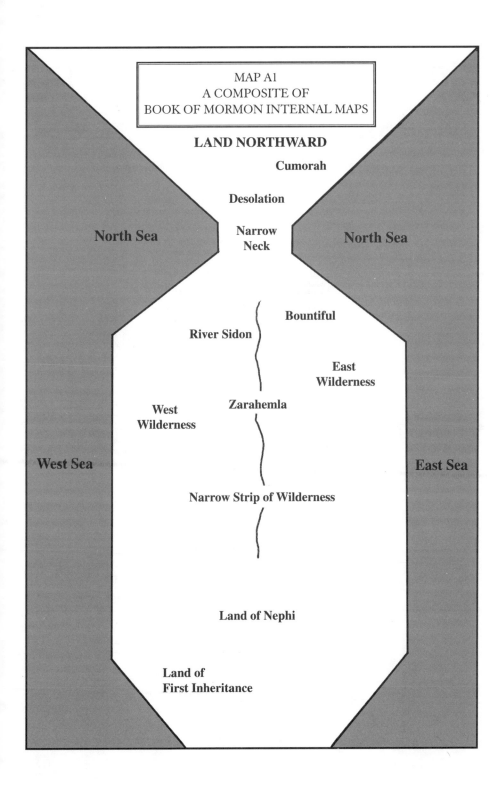

MAP A1
A COMPOSITE OF
BOOK OF MORMON INTERNAL MAPS

LAND NORTHWARD

Cumorah

Desolation

Narrow
Neck

North Sea

North Sea

Bountiful

River Sidon

East
Wilderness

Zarahemla

West
Wilderness

West Sea

East Sea

Narrow Strip of Wilderness

Land of Nephi

Land of
First Inheritance

Table A1
Internal Maps Comparisons

Feature:	Layton, 1939	Washburn, 1939	Ludlow, 1981	Nielson, 1987	Proctor, 1988
Hill Cumorah and narrow neck	Hill Cumorah not specified	Hill Cumorah above narrow neck	Hill Cumorah not specified	Hill Cumorah above narrow neck	Hill Cumorah above the narrow neck
River Sidon empties into sea on north	Empties into sea east of neck	Empties into sea east of narrow neck	Empties into sea west of narrow neck	Empties into sea west of narrow neck	Empties into sea east of narrow neck
Seas	Sea (on north) Sea west, sea east	West sea, East sea	North Sea (both sides of neck) , West Sea, East Sea	West Sea, East Sea	sea north, sea west, sea east, sea south
Wilderness areas	West sea area and narrow strip of wilderness	Wilderness of Hermounts, north and west of Sidon	Wilderness of Hermounts, East and South wilderness areas	Wilderness of Hermounts, west east, and south wilderness areas	west, east, and south wilderness areas
Cities in east sea area	Moroni, Nephihah, Lehi, Moriantum, Omner, Gid, Mulek	Moroni, Aaron, Nephihah, Lehi, Moriantum, Omner, Gid, Mulek	Nephihah, Antionum, Moroni, Jershon, Lehi, Moriantun, Gid, Omner, Mulek	Moroni, Nephihah, Aaron, Lehi, Morianton, Omner, Gid, Mulek	Jershon, Antionum, Moroni, Nephihah, Aaron, Mulek, City Bountiful, Gid, Omner, Lehi, Morianton
Cities in west sea area	(Alma 53:8,22; Alma 52:15)	Zeezrom, Cumeni, Antiparah	Zeezrom, Cumeni, Antiparah	Judea, Antiparah, Cumeni, Zeezrom, Ishmael, Ani-Anti, Middoni, Jerusalem	Antiparah, Judea, Jerusalem, Ani-Anti
Cities/lands east River Sidon	Jershon, Judea, Antionum, Manti	Gideon, Antionum, Siron, Minon, Aaron, Manti	Gideon, Hill Amnihu, Aaron	Jershon, Hill Onidah, Antionum, Hill Amnihu, Gideon	Hill Amnihu, Gideon Valley, Gideon, Manti
Cities/lands west River Sidon	Hermounts north and west of Sidon	Jershon, Sidom, Aaron, Ammonihah, Noah, Melek, Judea	Sidom, Ammonihah, Noah, Judea, Minon, Melek, Manti	Noah, Ammonihah, Aaron, Sidom, Melek, Minon, Manti	Jacobugath, Ammonihah, Noah, Sidom, Melek, Minon, Cumeni, Zeezrom
Cities in south, land of Nephi	none specified	Helam, Amulon Mormon, Ani-Anti, Jerusalem, Shilom, Shemlon, Middoni, Midian, Shimnilon, Ishmael, Lemuel	Amulon, Helam, Middoni, Shilom Midian, Mormon, Jerusalem, Ishmael, Shemlon, Lemuel, Shimnilon	Helam, Mormon, Midian, Shilom, Shemlon, Amulon, Lemuel, Shemnilon	Helam, Middoni, Siron, Shemlon, Shilom, Shimnilon, Amulon, Mormon, Midian, Ishmael

Mesoamerican Maps

Mesoamerica is the most popular area today where Book of Mormon events are thought to have taken place. The reason for this is largely historical, dating from the days in Nauvoo when the Saints became excited over the ruins found by Stephens and Catherwood. However, today proponents of the Mesoamerican setting recognize that the original excitement was over ruins of a post-Nephite civilization. Still, interest in the area is supported by new interpretations.

Map A2, presented on the following page, is a generalization of points of geography taken from the works of those who today propose a Mesoamerican setting for the Book of Mormon. Some differences in interpretation exist, notably in a choice for the River Sidon and for directions based upon a choice of seas. Immediately following Map A2 is Map A3, a simplified map of present-day Mesoamerica showing a few locations that allows readers to make some comparisons with Map A2.

Map A2 is a composite made from the maps of four geographers, John Sorenson, F. Richard Hauck, Joseph Allen and David Palmer. Areas of general agreement are indicated on Map A2. The works of these authors have been studied and, where appropriate, the results are presented in Table A2, following Map A3. While other maps have been suggested over the years, the works of these four authors are probably representative of the most recent.

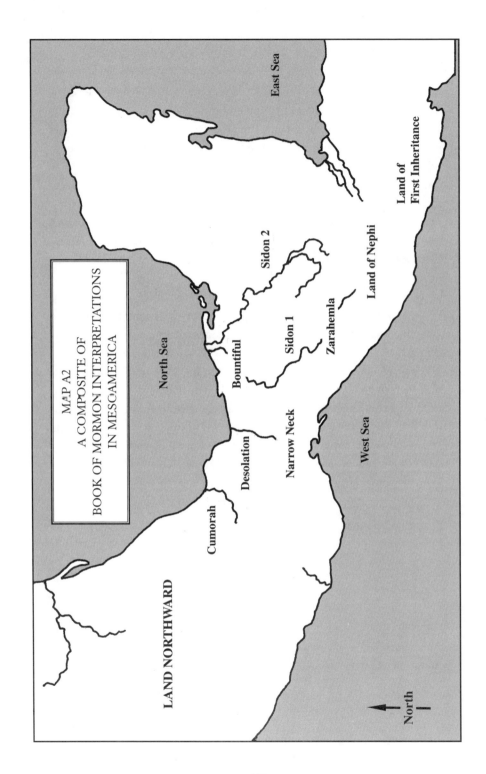

MAP A2
A COMPOSITE OF
BOOK OF MORMON INTERPRETATIONS
IN MESOAMERICA

East Sea

Land of
First Inheritance

Sidon 2

North Sea

Land of Nephi

Bountiful

Sidon 1

Zarahemla

Desolation

Narrow Neck

West Sea

Cumorah

LAND NORTHWARD

North

174

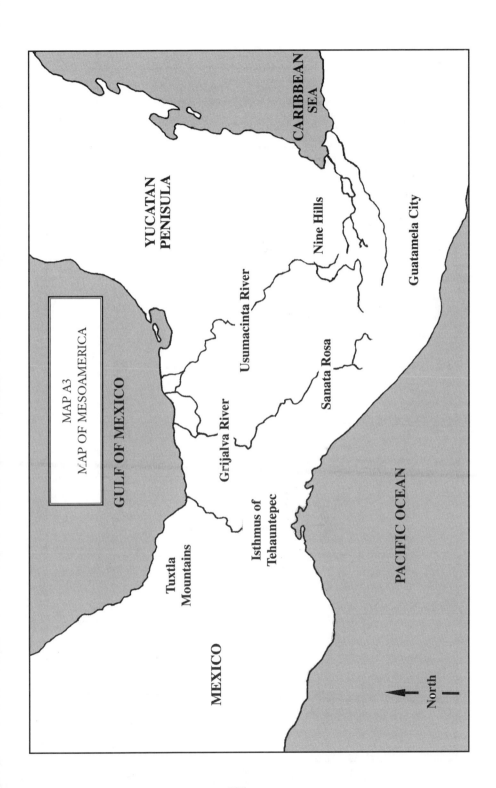

MAP A3
MAP OF MESOAMERICA

GULF OF MEXICO

YUCATAN
PENISULA

CARIBBEAN
SEA

MEXICO

Tuxtla
Mountains

Isthmus of
Tehauntepec

Grijalva River

Usumacinta River

Nine Hills

Sanata Rosa

Guatamela City

PACIFIC OCEAN

North

Table A2 Mesoamerican Maps Comparisons				
Feature:	Sorenson, 1986	Hauck, 1988	Allen, 1989	Palmer, 1992
Choice for River Sidon	Sidon 1 (Grijalava River)	Sidon 2 (Usumacinta River)	Sidon 1 (Grijalava River)	Sidon 1 (Grijalava River)
Land of Desolation	Above narrow neck of land (Isthmus of Tehauntepec	Coastal area, Southern Isthmus of Tehauntepec	Above narrow neck land (Isthmus of of Tehauntepec)	Above narrow neck of land (Isthmus of Tehauntepec)
Seas	East Sea (Gulf of Mexico) West Sea (Pacific Ocean)	East Sea (Carribean Sea) West Sea (Pacific Ocean) North Sea (Gulf of Mexico) South Sea (Pacific Ocean)	Sea East (Carribean Sea) Sea West (Pacific Ocean)	East Sea (Gulf of Mexico) West Sea (Pacific Ocean)
Hill Cumorah	Above the narrow neck in Tuxtla mountains	Above the narrow neck in Tuxtla mountains	Above the narrow neck in Tuxtla mountains	Above the narrow neck in Tuxtla mountains
Land of Zarahemla	Associated with Sidon 1, Southern head	Associated with Sidon 2, Southern head	Associated with Sidon 1, Southern head	Associated with Sidon 1, Southern head
Yucatan Peninsula	No Book of Mormon lands proposed on Peninsula	No Book of Mormon lands proposed on Peninsula	Land of Bountiful; Cities on the east by the sea	No Book of Mormon lands proposed on Peninsula
Land of Nephi	Area of Guatemala City	Area of Guatemala City	Area of Guatemala City	Area of Guatemala City
Land northward	Above isthmus, in southern Mexico	Above isthmus in southern Mexico	Above isthmus in southern Mexico	Above isthmus in southern Mexico
Land of Bountiful	At Isthmus of Tehauntepec	Southwest Carribean seashore	Southern regions of Yucatan Peninsula	At Isthmus of Tehauntepec
Attempts to correlate cities with archaeological sites	Santa Rosa (city of Zarahemla), Kaminaljuyu near Guatamala City (city of Nephi), etc.	Nine Hills (city of Zarahemla), Kaminaljuyu near Guatamala City (city of Nephi), etc.	Santa Rosa (city of Zarahemla), Kaminaljuyu near Guatamala City (city of Nephi), etc.	Santa Rosa (city of Zarahemla), Kaminaljuyu near Guatamala City (city of Nephi), etc.

Great Lakes Maps

Early in the history of the Church, the Great Lakes area of the United States was originally thought to be the Book of Mormon lands where both the Jaredites and the Lamanites fought their last battles at Hill Cumorah. But only recently have some attempts been made to place the setting for the Book of Mormon in the Great Lakes area of the United States and Canada.

In 1983 Vernal Holley suggested that names found in eastern United States and Canada may have had Book of Mormon connections. His map indicates a narrow neck of land at Niagara, and Lakes Ontario and Erie are suggested as the East and West seas mentioned in the Book of Mormon.

In 1993 Delbert Curtis published *Christ in North America* in which he proposed that Book of Mormon events took place in lands in close proximity to the narrow neck of land, located at the Niagara River in western New York.

Map A4, presented on the following page, is a simplified version of Map A found on the inside front cover of this book. It is presented here because it is probably the most complete Great Lakes map presented thus far that seems to consistently meet Book of Mormon specifications. Map A5, presented on the page following Map A4, is a map of the eastern Great Lakes area with a few locations indicated to help readers make comparisons with Map A4.

Table A3, presented on the page following Map A5, makes some comparisons between features of geography taken from the works of Duane Aston, the works of Delbert Curtis and from the works of Vernal Holley.

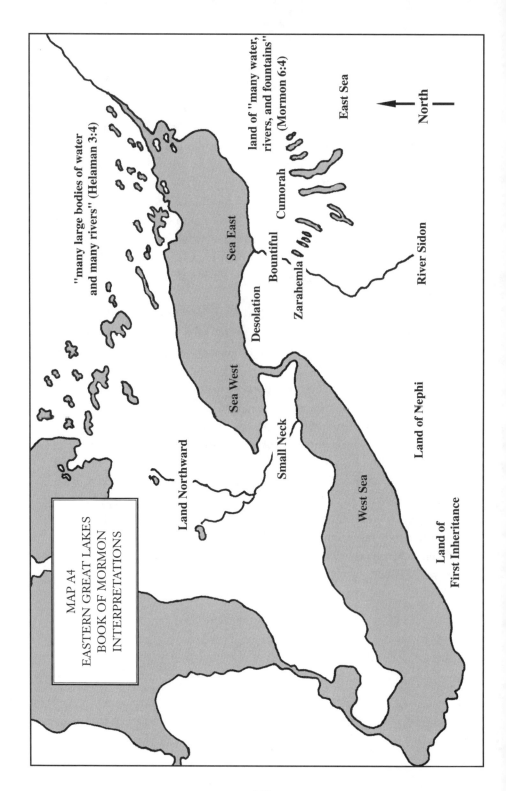

MAP A4
EASTERN GREAT LAKES
BOOK OF MORMON
INTERPRETATIONS

"many large bodies of water
and many rivers" (Helaman 3:4)

land of "many water,
rivers, and fountains"
(Mormon 6:4)

East Sea

North

Sea East

Desolation

Bountiful

Cumorah

Zarahemla

River Sidon

Sea West

Land of Nephi

Land Northward

Small Neck

West Sea

Land of
First Inheritance

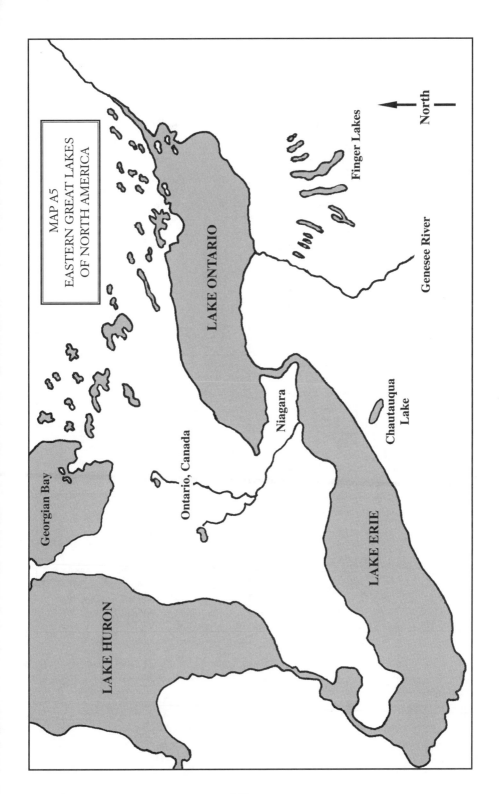

MAP A5
EASTERN GREAT LAKES
OF NORTH AMERICA

LAKE HURON

Georgian Bay

LAKE ONTARIO

Ontario, Canada

Niagara

LAKE ERIE

Chautauqua Lake

Finger Lakes

Genesee River

North

Table A3 Great Lakes Maps Comparisons			
Feature:	**Aston, 1998**	**Curtis, 1993**	**Holley, 1983**
Narrow neck of land	Small neck at Niagara	Small neck at Niagara	None identified
Hill Cumorah	Western New York	Western New York	Not identified
Seas	East Sea (Cayuga Lake) West Sea (Lake Erie) Sea east (Lake Ontario) Sea west (Lake Ontario) West sea south (Lake Erie)	Sea east (Lake Ontario) Sea west (Lake Erie)	Sea East (Lake Ontario) Sea West (Lake Erie)
Land northward	South western shores of Lake Ontario; Northward in Ontario Providence, Canada	Northward in Ontario Providence, Canada	Lands northward in Ontario Providence, Canada
River Sidon	Genesee River	Niagara River	Genesee River
Land of Desolation	Southern shores of Lake Ontario	East of the Niagara River	None
Land of Bountiful	Wilderness area south of Lake Ontario, rich in wildlife	Southeastern Niagara River area, in New York	None
Land of Nephi	Centered in the Lake Chautauqua area	South west of the Finger Lakes, eastward from head of the Niagara River	Lehi-Delaware Rivers area
Land of Zarahemla	Central Genesee River area	Northern Niagara River area	Northern Genesee River area
Attempts to correlate with archaeological sites	Maps of Indian settlements; Archaeological sites along southern shore or Lake Ontario	Archaeological sites along southern shore of Lake Ontario	None

Partial Bibliography

Adair, James, *The History of the American Indians* (New York: Johnson Reprint Corp., 1968).

Allen, Joseph, *Exploring the Lands of the Book of Mormon* (Orem: SA Publishers, 1989).

Arden, Harvey, *National Geographic* Magazine, September 1987.

Bauchamp, William, *A History of the New York Iroquois* (Fort Washington: Ira J. Friedman, 1968).

Book of Mormon Student Manual (Religion 121 and 122) (Salt Lake City: Church of Jesus Christ of Latter-day Saints, 1989).

Curtis, Delbert W., *Christ in North America* (Tigard: Resource Communications, Inc., 1993).

Dialogue: A Journal of Mormon Thought, vol. 23, No.1, Spring 1990.

Dow, Charles Mason, vol. 1 *Anthology and Bibliography of Niagara Falls* (Albany: State of New York, J.S. Lyon Co., 1921).

Dragoo, Don W., *Mounds for the Dead: An Analysis of the Adena Culture* (Pittsburgh: Annals of the Carnegie Museum, 1963).

Epigraphic Society Occasional Publications (San Diego: The Epigraphic Society).

Fagan, Brian M., *Ancient North America* (London: Thames & Hudson, 1991).

F.A.R.M.S., *Reexploring the Book of Mormon* (Salt Lake City: Deseret Book and FARMS, 1992), 187.

F.A.R.M.S., *The Geography of Book of Mormon Events: A Source Book* (John Sorenson, 1990).

F.A.R.M.S., *Review of Books on the Book of Mormon* vol.1 (Provo: F.A.R.M.S., 1989).

F.A.R.M.S., SP-WER, Sydney Sperry, "Were There Two Cumorahs?", 1983.

Gallatin, Albert, *Synopsis of the Indian Tribes* (New York: AMS Press, 1836).

Haines, Elijah M., *The American Indian* (Chicago: The Massinnagan Co., 1888).

Hauck, F. Richard, *Deciphering the Geography of the Book of Mormon* (Salt Lake City: Deseret Book Co., 1988).

Henry, Thomas, *The Wilderness Messiah: The Story of Hiawatha and the Iroquois* (New York: William Sloan Associates, 1955).

Howard, Robert W., *The Horse in America* (Chicago: Follett Publishing Co., 1965).

Jessee, Dean C., *The Papers of Joseph Smith,* vol.1 (Salt Lake City: Deseret Book Co., 1989).

Ketchum, William, *An Authentic and Comprehensive History of Buffalo* (Buffalo: Rockwell, Baker, and Hill, Printers, 1864).

Mallory, Arlington, *Lost America* (Washington DC: Overlook Book Co., 1951).

McConkie, Bruce R., *Mormon Doctrine* (Salt Lake City: Bookcraft, 1966).

McClone, William R. and Phillip M. Leonard, *Ancient Celtic America* (Fresno: Panorama West Books, 1986).

McGavin, Cecil E. and Willard Bean, *Geography of the Book of Mormon* (Salt Lake City: Bookcraft, 1949).

McIntosh, John, *The Origins of the North American Indians* (McGavin & Bean, chapter 1).

Morrison's Annals of Western New York (Ovid: W.E. Morrison & Co., 1975).

Monson, Thomas (*Ensign*, Conference issue, October, 1990).

Nibley, Hugh, *An Approach to the Book of Mormon* (Salt Lake City: The Church of Jesus Christ of Latter-day Saints, Melchizedek

Priesthood Quorums, 1957).

Nishenko, S.P. and G.A. Bollinger, "Forecasting Damaging Earthquakes in Central and Eastern United States," *Science*, vol. 249, 21 September, 1990.

Palmer, David A., *In Search of Cumorah* (Bountiful: Horizon Publishers & Distributors, 1981,1992).

Reaman, George E., *The Trial of the Iroquois Indians* (Tronto: Peter Martin Associates, 1967).

Reynolds, George and Janne Sjodahl, *Commentary on the Book of Mormon* (Salt Lake City: Deseret News Press, 1955).

Ritchie, William, *The Archaeology of New York State* (Garden City: The Natural History Press, 1965).

Roberts, Brigham H., *Studies on the Book of Mormon* (Urbana, Chicago: University of Illinois Press, 1985).

Schoolcraft, Henry R., *The Indian Tribes of the United States*, vol.1 (Philadelphia: J.S. Lippincott & Co., 1885).

Schoolcraft, Henry R., *Notes on the Iroquois* (Milford: Kraus Reprint Co., 1975).

Sertima, Ivan Van, *They Came Before Columbus* (New York: Random House, 1976).

Shetrone, H.C., *The Mound Builders* (Washington, N.Y.: Kennikat Press, 1930).

Smith, Joseph, *History of the Church,* vol. 2, (Salt Lake City: Deseret Book, 1978).

Smith, Joseph Fielding, *Doctrines of Salvation*, vol. 2, (Salt Lake City, Bookcraft, 1956).

Sheele, Raymond, *Warfare of the Iroquois and Their Neighbors* (Ann Arbor: University Microfilms, 1980). This book is Sheele's Ph.D.. Doctoral Dissertation, Columbia University, 1950.

Sorenson, John L., *An Ancient American Setting for the Book Of Mormon* (Salt Lake City: Deseret Book Co., 1985).

Stephens, John Lloyd, *Incidents of Travel in Central America, Chiapas, and Yucatn*. Two volumes, illustrated by Frederick Catherwood (New York: Dover Publications, Inc., 1969).

Talmage, James E., *Articles of Faith* (Salt Lake City: The Church of Jesus Christ of Latter-day Saints, 1952).

Thelin, Gail P. and Richard J. Pike, U.S. Geological Survey, 1991, Digital Shaded-Relief Portrayal Map I-2206.

Thomas, Cyrus, *Mound Explorations*, 1893.

Thomas, Cyrus, *Twelfth Annual Report on the Mound Explorations* (Washington, D.C.: Bureau of Ethnology, 1894).

Thompson, Gunner, *American Discovery* (Seattle: Argonauts Misty Isles Press, 1992).

Thompson, John H., *Geography of New York State* (Syracuse: University Press, 1966).

Turner, O., *Pioneer History of the Holland Purchase of Western New York* (McGavin & Bean, chapter 1).

Wallace, Paul A., *Indians in Pennsylvania* (Harrisburg: The Pennsylvania Historical and Museum Commission, 1989).

Wheeler-Voegelin, Ermine, *Indians of Ohio and Indiana Prior to 1795*, vol.1 (New York: Garland Publishing Inc., 1974).

Young, Brigham, *Journal of Discourses*, vol. 93, 38.

Appendix C

References:
Geography, Cities, Lands of Map A

AARON
• Alma journeyed toward the city Aaron (Alma 8:13) • Alma departed out of Ammoniaha toward Aaron; returned by another way, which was on the south of Ammonihah (Alma 8:18) • Foundation for city (Nephihah) joining the borders of Aaron and Moroni (Alma 50:14)

ALMA, VALLEY
• Alma, from land of Helam, traveled all day, arrived at the valley of Alma; then 12 more days they arrived in Zarahemla (Mosiah 24:20, 25)

AMMONIHAH
• 3 days journey north of city of Melek (Alma 8:6) • Alma journeyed towards the city of Aaron (Alma 8:13) • Alma returned by another way, by the way which is on the south of the city (Alma 8:18) • Lamanites had come in upon the "wilderness side" into the borders of the land (Alma 16:2) • Came out into the land of Sidom; Amulek came "over" to the land of Zarahemla (Alma 15:18) • In the borders of the land of Zarahemla (Alma 25:2)

AMNIHU, HILL
• Hill Amnihu was east of the River Sidon, which ran by the land of Zarahemla (Alma 2:15)

AMULON

• Amulon and Lamanites traveling in the wilderness in search of the land of Nephi discovered the land of Helam; asked Alma to show them way to Nephi (Mosiah 23:35, 36) • Amulon appointed teacher over land of Shemlon, Shilom, and Amulon (Mosiah 24:1) • Seed of Amulon fled into east wilderness Alma (24:24)

ANI-ANTI

• A village "over" from city of Jerusalem; from there "over" to the land of Middoni (Alma 21:12)

ANTIONUM

• East by the land of Zarahemla; nearly bordering upon the seashore which was south of the land of Jershon, which also bordered upon the wilderness south (Alma 31:3) • Departed out of land of Antionum into the wilderness, and took journey "round about" in the wilderness, away by the head of the River Sidon, into the land of Manti (Alma 43:22)

ANTIPARAH

• A neighboring city, from Judea, to which Helaman marched as if going to the city beyond in the borders by the seashore (Alma 56;31) • Helaman fled northward, Lamanites in pursuit; fled 3 days; capture Antiparah; prisoners sent to Zarahemla (Alma 56:36, 42, 51, 57)

BOUNTIFUL

• Bordered upon the land Desolation; it being the wilderness which is filled with all manner of wild animals of every kind (Alma 22:30, 31) • Bountiful from the "east to the west sea" (Alma 22:33)

CUMENI

• Close by to Judea; prisoners sent "down" to Zarahemla (Alma 57:11, 15, 16)

DESOLATION

• It being so far northward (Alma 22:30) • Land Desolation by the narrow pass which led into the land northward (Alma 50:34)

GIDEON VALLEY

• Alma pursued Amlicites from Hill Amnihu, to valley of Gideon (Alma 2:20) • Departed out of the valley of Gideon towards the city of Zarahemla (Alma 2:26) • Alma leaves Zarahemla, went upon east of River

Sidon, into the valley of Gideon, where city of Gideon was (Alma 6:7) • Land of Gideon southward away to the land of Manti (Alma 17:1)

GID

• Gid in city chain in east borders by the seashore: Lehi, Morianton, Omner, Gid, Mulek (Alma 51:26) • Nephite prisoners guarded in city of Gid; after taking city of Gid, Moroni took Lamanite prisoners to city Bountiful (Alma 55:26)

HELAM

• Alma departed into wilderness, journeyed 8 days in wilderness; came to "very beautiful and pleasant land, a land of pure water" (Mosiah 23:3, 4) • Amulon and Lamanites traveling in wilderness in search of land of Nephi discovered land of Helam (Mosiah 23:35).

HERMOUNTS

• Toward the wilderness which was west and north... Lamanites scattered on the west and on the north to Hermounts; infested by wild and ravenous beasts (Alma 2:37, 38)

ISHMAEL

• Ammon, met Alma in Gideon; Ammon entered the land of Ishmael (Alma 17:19) • Tended king's flocks in "water of Sebus"; a place of water (Alma 17:26,31) • Lord told Ammon to "go up" to land of Nephi; it was "down" to the land of Middoni (Alma 20:2, 7)

JERSHON

• On the east by the sea (which joins land Bountiful), on the south of the land Bountiful (Alma 27:22) • People of Ammon went "down" (from south) to Jershon (Alma 27:26) • Korihor came "over" to land of Jershon; carried out of land, came "over" into land of Gideon (Alma 30:19, 21)

JERUSALEM

• Away joining the borders of Mormon (Alma 21:1) • The land of their fathers' nativity, joining the borders of Mormon (Alma 21:1,2)

JUDEA

• Helaman marched with 2,000 young soldiers in support of the people in the borders of the land on the south by the west sea (Alma 53:22) • Helaman arrives in Judea (Alma 56:9)

LEHI-NEPHI
   • "Up" from the land of Zarahemla; wander 40 days, came to hill, north of Shilom; then went "down into the land of Nephi" (Mosiah 7:1, 4, 5, 7) • Associated with the city of Shilom (Mosiah 7:21) • Associated with the land of Shilom (Mosiah 9:6, 8)

LEHI
   • In the north by the borders of the seashore (Alma 50:15) • Joined the borders of the land of Morinaton (Alma 50:25)

LINE
   • Day and a half journey for a Nephite, on the "line" Bountiful and the land of Desolation (Alma 22:32) • Fortifying the "line" between the Nephites and the Lamanites, between the land of Zarahemla and the land of Nephi, from the west sea, running by the head of the River Sidon—the Nephites possessing all the land northward, yea, even all the land which was northward of the land of Bountiful (Alma 50:11) • A day's journey on the "line" which they had fortified (Helaman 4:7)

LINE OF POSSESSION
   • The line between the Nephites and the Lamanites, between the land of Zarahemla and the land of Nephi, running from the west sea, running by the head of the River Sidon, the Nephites possessing all the land which was northward of the land Bountiful (Alma 50:11)

MANTI
   • Lamanites departed out of land of Antionum into the wilderness away by the head of the River Sidon that they might come into the land of Manti (Alma 43:22) • Part of armies of Moroni concealed on the east; remainder in the west valley, on the west of River Sidon, down into the borders of the land of Manti (Alma 43:32) • The wilderness side, which was near to the city (Alma 58:13) • Having traveled much in the wilderness towards the land of Zarahemla (Alma 58:23) • Lamanites fled to land of Nephi (Alma 58:38)

MELEK
   • On the west of the River Sidon, on the west by the borders of the wilderness (Alma 8:3) • 3 days journey on the north of the land of Melek, came to the city of Ammonihah (Alma 8:6) • Melek near Zarahemla (Alma 31:6) • People of Ammon departed from land of Jershon and came "over" to the land of Melek (Alma 35:13)

MIDDONI

• Ammon to go "down" (from Ishmael) to Middoni (Alma 20:7) • Aaron came "over" from city of Jerusalem to village of Ani-Anti; from there he came "over" into the land of Middoni (Alma 21:12) • From land of Nephi it was down to Middoni; • King, in Nephi, questioned why Ammon had not come "up" out of Middoni (Alma 22:3)

MIDIAN

• Ammon came "forth" to land of Midian, and then to the land of Ishmael (Alma 24:5)

MINON

• "Above" (higher elevation) the land of Zarahemla, in the course of the land of Nephi (Alma 2:24)

MORIANTON

• Joined the borders of Lehi; both which were on the borders of the seashore (Alma 50:25) • People fled to the borders of the land Desolation…by the narrow pass which led to the land northward, by the sea, on the west and on the east (Alma 50:34)

MORMON

• In the borders of the land having been infested by times or seasons, by wild beasts; in Mormon a fountain of pure water; "waters of Mormon" (Mosiah 18:4,5) • Waters of Mormon; in the forest that was near the place of Mormon, the waters of Mormon, the forest of Mormon (Mosiah 18:30) • In the borders of Nephi (Alma 5:3)

MORONI

• By the "east sea," on the south, by the line of possessions of the Lamanites (Alma 50:13) • In the borders by the seashore (Alma 51:22) • Those who fled out of city of Moroni came to city of Nephihah (Alma 51:24) • Strongly fortified (Alma 51:27) • In the borders by the seashore (Alma 62:25) • Land of Moroni by the wilderness south, and in the borders by the wilderness on the east (Alma 62:34) • Lamanites in Moroni encircled about in the borders by the wilderness on the south and in the borders by the wilderness on the east (Alma 62:34)

MULEK

• On east borders by the seashore (Alma 51:26) • Lamanites marching in the north, abandoned their design in marching into the land northward and retreated to the city of Mulek (Alma 52:2) • Plains between city of Bountiful and Mulek (Alma 52:20) • Wilderness on west of city of Mulek (Alma 52:22) • Teancum retreated down by the seashore, north-ward (Alma 52:23) • Lamanites wearied of their long march toward the city of Bountiful (Alma 52:31) • Mulek one of the strongest holds of Lamanites in the land of Nephi (Alma 53:6)

NARROW STRIP OF WILDERNESS

• Sea on the east and on the west, and which was divided from the land of Zarahemla by a narrow strip of wilderness...round about on the borders of the seashore; on the borders of the wilderness on the north by land of Zarahemla; through the borders of Manti by the head of River Sidon, running from the east towards the west, dividing Nephites and Lamanites (Alma 22:27)

NECK OF LAND

• "Small" neck of land (Alma 22:32)

NEPHI

• Or, of the land of our fathers' first inheritance (Mosiah 9:1) • Away on the "south" of the land of Shilom, watering flocks (Mosiah 9:14) • Sent spies out round about the land of Shemlon; came upon the "north" of the land of Shilom (Mosiah 10:7) • "Up" from the land of Shemlon (Mosiah 20:7) • Alma journeying south away from the land of Gideon met sons of Mosiah. They had been "up" to the land of Nephi (Alma 17:1, 8) • Departed Zarahemla to go "up" to the land of Nephi (Alma 17:7) • Ammon should not go "up" to land of Nephi (from Ishmael?) (Alma 20:2) • Aaron in land of Nephi; "up" out of Middoni (Alma 22:3) • Land of Nephi did run in a straight course from the east sea to the west (Alma 50:8)

NEPHIHAH

• Between Moroni and Aaron (Alma 50:14) • People from Moroni came to Nephihah (Alma 51:24) • Cross head of Sidon "over" to the city of Nephihah (Alma 56:25) • People of Nephihah who were gathered together from the city of Moroni, Lehi and Morianton (Alma 59:5) • Lamanites flee from the land of Manti, came "over" and joined Lamanites near Nephihah (Alma 59:6) • Moroni and Pahoran took march towards land of Nephihah; send Lamanites to dwell with people of Ammon (in Antionum?); pursued march toward Nephihah; Plains of Nephihah, near the city (Alma 62:14, 17, 18, 19) • Moroni went forth from the land of Nephihah to the land of Lehi (Alma 62:30)

NOAH

• Near the borders of the wilderness (Alma 16:3,4)

ONIDAH, HILL

• Hill Onidah not far from Jershon? (Alma 32:4) • Amulek finished speaking on hill Onidah and "came over" into land of Jershon (Alma 35:1) • Amalickiah fled into wilderness and went "up" into the land of Nephi, from Land Northward; he went to "place" which was called Onidah, to where the Lamanites had fled—to the place of arms; later he marched to the land of Nephi (Alma 47:1, 5, 20)

OTHER CITIES

• Lemuel, Shimnilon (Alma 23:12) • Moronihah, Gilgal, Onihah, Mocum, Gadiandi, Gadiomnah, Gimgimno, Jacoburath, Laman, Josh, Gad, Kiskumen (3 Nephi, Chap.9)

SEA, EAST, WEST

• Narrow strip of wilderness, which ran from the sea east even to the sea west (Alma 22:27) • Lamanites on the east, by the seashore (Alma 22:29) • Nephites inhabited Bountiful from the east unto the west sea (Alma 22:33) • Land of Nephi run in a straight course from the east sea to the west (Alma 50:8) • Moroni drove Lamanites out of east wilderness, which was north of their own possessions; caused inhabitants in land of Zarahemla and in the land round about to go forth into the east wilderness, even to the borders by the seashore and possess the land (Alma 50:9) • From the west sea, running by the head of River Sidon (Alma 50:11) • Cities of Lehi, Morianton, Omner, Gid, Mulek, all on east borders by the seashore (Alma 51:26)

SEBUS

• A place of water (near Ishmael) (Alma 17:26-43) • Lamanite practice to scatter flocks (Alma 18:7) • Ammon was to go "up" to land of Nephi (from land of Ishmael) (Alma 20:2)

SHEMLON, SHILOM

• Ammon traveled "up" to land of Lehi-Nephi; wandered 40 days in wilderness, came to hill, north of land of Shilom (Mosiah 7:5) • Land of Nephi, away on the south of land of Shilom (Mosiah 9:14) • Sent spies

out "round about" the land of Shemlon (Mosiah 10:7) • High tower to
overlook the land of Shilom and Shemlon (Mosiah 11:12) • Built a great
tower on hill "north" of Shilom (Mosiah 11:13) • Limhi and people left
city of Nephi and went into wilderness; traveled "around" the land of
Shilom; went "round about" in wilderness and "bent" course toward
Zarahemla; many days in wilderness (Mosiah 22:8,11,13)

SHIPS
• Launched by the land Desolation, into the west sea, by the narrow
neck which led into the land northward (Alma 63:5)

SIDOM
• Departed out of Ammonihah; came to land of Sidom; came over to
land of Zarahemla (Alma 15:1,18)

WILDERNESS
• Wilderness side to Ammonihah (Alma 16:2) • South wilderness,
which was on the east side of the River Sidon (Alma 16:7) • On the west,
in the land of Nephi; west of the land of Zarahemla, in the borders by the
seashore; on the west in the land of Nephi in the place of their father's
first inheritance, bordering along by the seashore (Alma 22:28) •
Nephite possession of all land bordering on the wilderness at the head of
the River Sidon, from east to the west, round about on the wilderness
side; on the north, even until them came to the land they called Bountiful
(Alma 22:29) • People of Ammon came to the wilderness which divided
the land of Nephi from the land of Zarahemla; came to borders of land
(of Zarahemla) (Alma 27:14) • Drove Lamanites in east wilderness into
their own lands, which were south of the land of Zarahemla (Alma 50:7)

ZARAHEMLA
• From the city of Zarahemla, went "over" upon the east of the River
Sidon, into the valley and city of Gideon (Alma 6:7)

ZEEZROM
• A city in the southeast, near Manti (Alma 56:14)

Index

A

B

C

D

E

F

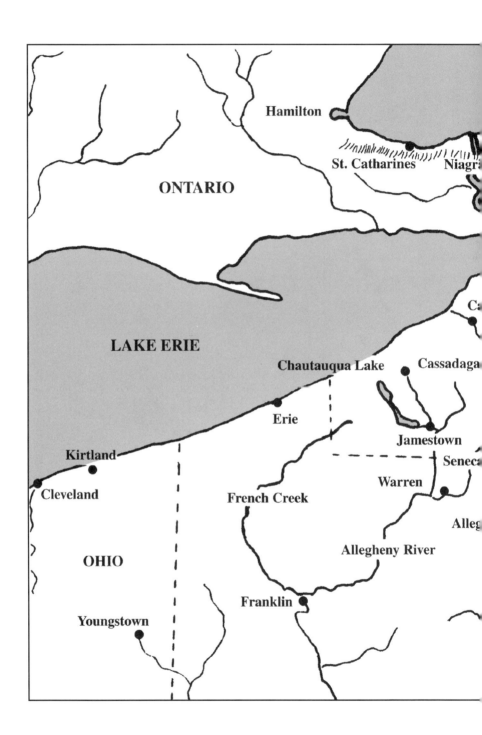

MAP B